GUARANTEED TO FAIL

GUARANTEED TO FAIL

Fannie Mae, Freddie Mac and the Debacle of Mortgage Finance

With a New Chapter on
'Government-sponsored Enterprises and India'

Viral V. Acharya
Matthew Richardson Stijn Van Nieuwerburgh
Lawrence J. White

HARPER
BUSINESS

First published in 2011 by Princeton University Press, New Jersey, US

First published in India in 2011 by Collins Business
An imprint of HarperCollins *Publishers*
A-75, Sector 57, Noida, Uttar Pradesh 201301, India
www.harpercollins.co.in

This edition published in India in 2018 by Harper Business

2 4 6 8 10 9 7 5 3

ISBN: 978-93-5029-065-1

Printed and bound at
Replika Press Pvt. Ltd.

TO OUR FAMILIES AND PARENTS

CONTENTS

ACKNOWLEDGMENTS

Many insights presented in this book were generated during research on two earlier books that the four of us contributed to at NYU-Stern: *Restoring Financial Stability: How to Repair a Failed System* (Wiley, March 2009); and *Regulating Wall Street: The Dodd-Frank Act and the New Architecture of Global Finance* (Wiley, October 2010). We owe much to all of our colleagues who contributed to those books, especially those who contributed to the chapters on the government-sponsored enterprises (GSEs): Dwight Jaffee (who was visiting Stern during 2008–9), T. Sabri Oncu (also visiting Stern during 2008–10), and Bob Wright. We received valuable feedback on the first draft of the book from Heitor Almeida, Ralph Koijen, and Amit Seru; useful expositional comments from Sanjay Agarwal, Les Levi, and Manjiree Jog; and excellent research assistance from Vikas Singh on how countries other than the United States deal with home ownership and mortgage markets. We would like to thank Robert Collender, principal policy analyst at the Federal Housing Finance Agency (FHFA), for helping us better understand the FHFA data. We are also grateful to the professionalism of the staff at Princeton University Press, especially Seth Ditchik, who managed the process for us right from the book proposal to eventual publication. Finally, we owe substantial gratitude to a number of economists, policy makers, and practitioners—some named in the book and others unnamed—who have over the past two decades studied the GSEs, with prescience pointed out the flaws in their design, and warned of the likely adverse consequences due these flaws. Their collective wisdom has shaped our understanding of the GSEs in significant measure and helped us provide original recommendations for much-needed reform of mortgage finance in the United States.

PROLOGUE

> The shapers of the American mortgage finance system hoped to achieve the security of government ownership, the integrity of local banking and the ingenuity of Wall Street. Instead they got the ingenuity of government, the security of local banking and the integrity of Wall Street.
>
> —*David Frum (columnist, and former speechwriter for President George W. Bush),* National Post, *July 11, 2008*

On September 30, 1999, a *New York Times* reporter, Steven Holmes, published a piece titled "Fannie Mae Eases Credit to Aid Mortgage Lending." The crux of the story was that Fannie Mae was lowering its credit standards, which in turn would increase home ownership. Franklin Raines, chief executive officer (CEO) of Fannie Mae at the time, is quoted in the article:

> Fannie Mae has expanded home ownership for millions of families in the 1990's by reducing down payment requirements. Yet there remain too many borrowers whose credit is just a notch below what our underwriting has required who have been relegated to paying significantly higher mortgage rates in the so-called subprime market.

Consistent with sound journalism, the story analyzed the potential consequences of Fannie Mae's foray into riskier lending. Quite presciently, the author Steven Holmes sounded an alarm that Fannie Mae was taking on large amounts of new risk, which in good times would not cause problems but in a downturn could lead to a massive government bailout. The article also quotes Peter Wallison, an American Enterprise Institute scholar and frequent critic of the government-sponsored enterprises (GSEs), in particular, the two largest ones, Fannie Mae and Freddie Mac:

> From the perspective of many people, including me, this is another thrift industry growing up around us. . . . If they fail, the government will have to step up and bail them out the way it stepped up and bailed out the thrift industry.

A decade later, we know how it all turned out: the worst financial crisis since the 1930s and bailouts so large that we no longer consider the savings and loan debacle to have been much of a financial crisis. This is not to argue that all of the blame should be placed on the doorstep of Fannie and Freddie. There is plenty of blame to go around at other large, complex financial institutions, including Bear Stearns, Lehman Brothers, Merrill Lynch, AIG, Wachovia, and Citigroup.

Nevertheless, Fannie and Freddie do deserve special attention. Currently, as of August 2010, the Treasury has injected a total of $148.2 billion into these entities. Yet it looks as if their financial health is not getting any better. Even putting aside all future foreclosures and portfolio losses, Fannie Mae and Freddie Mac are now sitting on more than 150,000 foreclosed homes. The Congressional Budget Office (CBO) projects that an additional $65 billion may be required to keep them afloat until 2019. The CBO has further estimated that the total taxpayer losses might ultimately reach the neighborhood of an astounding $350 billion.

Yet Fannie and Freddie barely register as news. In the most sweeping financial legislation since the 1930s, the Dodd-Frank

Wall Street Reform and Consumer Protection Act of 2010 barely mentions them, simply calling for a study of how to reform them.

Now there is a chance that the support that has been thrown at the banks—$550 billion of direct capital, $285 billion of loan guarantees, and insurance of $418 billion of assets—will be eventually paid off. In fact, some banks have repaid their loans with interest, albeit along a trail of real economic devastation. And even the poster child for financial excess, AIG, may be able to fully pay off the government if the housing market does not deteriorate further. But the chances are slim to none that either Fannie or Freddie will be able to pay back the funds. When the history of the crisis is all written, these institutions will turn out to be the most costly of the financial sector, and this sector includes some of the most tarnished financial institutions in America.

So where is the outrage?

There is no outrage because Fannie and Freddie have become a political football between the left and right wings of American politics. On the left, they were vehicles for promoting affordable housing for all, while on the right they furthered the idea of the ownership society. And they were a politician's dream: they reduced monthly mortgage costs without requiring any federal budgetary outlays.

Now that they have failed, and we have learned that the game has been costly indeed, conservative think tanks blame Fannie and Freddie for being ground zero of the subprime crisis. However, the liberal groups say that their role in the crisis is overblown and that it is simply a diversionary tactic away from what they consider to be the true causes of the housing bust: deregulation and the excesses of Wall Street. There is probably a little truth to both views. But these arguments are beside the point.

Fannie Mae and Freddie Mac are where they are because they were run as the largest hedge fund on the planet. A little calculation illustrates their business model.

Suppose that we offered you the following opportunity: We will invest $1, you lend us $39. With this $40, we will buy bank-originated pools of mortgages that are not easy to sell and face significant long-term risks. Although we will attempt to limit that risk by using sophisticated financial hedging instruments, our models have a significant potential for error and uncertainty. We will invest 15% of the funds in low-quality mortgages that households will be unable to pay in a recession or a severe housing downturn. And to make it even more interesting, we will become the largest financial institution in terms of assets that are related to mortgages and together buy around $1.7 trillion worth, making us truly too big to fail.

But it doesn't stop here. We are going to offer insurance on a whole lot more mortgages taken out in America, say $3.5 trillion (together), and guarantee them against default. We don't want much for offering this insurance—maybe around $.20 per $100.00 of mortgage—but that will provide us with $7 billion in profits per year (a figure that assumes absolutely zero foreclosures). As a lender to us, you might be worried how much capital we will hold as a buffer against all future defaults: for every $100 that we guarantee, we will hold only $.45. And because we want as big a market share as possible, we are going to backstop some dicey mortgages.

For this type of risky investment, we know that you are expecting a big return. However, we are going to pay you only the yield on government bonds plus a little extra. You would think our investment pitch was crazy and reject the deal outright. But if we came along and whispered to you that we have a wealthy uncle—his name is Sam—that will make you whole on the money that you lent us no matter what happens, do you care about the risk? If you believe that Sam will be there, you will give us your money freely.

This, of course, is a description of the business model of Fannie Mae and Freddie Mac. Put simply, they were *Guaranteed to Fail.* And it was a recipe for disaster for taxpayers. And unlike the banks or AIG, these risks were out in the open. Analysts have been pounding their fists on the table for years about them. Not only did each presidential administration not pull the plug;

it instead chose to extend the guarantees even further, passing on their risk to the next administration. In the process, each achieved its short-run goals of boosting consumption and spending by having households tap into their housing equity through first and second mortgages and home equity lines of credit. Being nowhere to be found on the government's books, the guarantees appeared to be a free lunch—until they weren't. As this Ponzi scheme of government guarantees has now ended, the misfortune of mopping up the mess has fallen on the current administration. How should it fix *Fannie Mae, Freddie Mac, and the Debacle of Mortgage Finance*?

Consider the scale and complexity of the problem. The government cannot simply default on the GSE debt with the intention of passing losses on to creditors. About 50% of this debt is held by financial institutions and about 20% by foreign investors, who also own the majority of government debt. Because of their size and interconnectedness, the GSEs cannot simply be unwound in the ways that have been successful for smaller financial firms. We are dealing with $3.5 trillion in mortgage guarantees, a $1.7 trillion mortgage portfolio, and a $2.2 trillion position in derivatives. Not only does the unwinding from the GSEs have to be handled well, but the Federal Reserve also has to plan its own exit from the $1.5 trillion position of GSE debt and GSE-backed securities that it accumulated as part of the rescue package for the economy. It is clear thus that any resolution to the problem of the GSEs will likely involve several years, if not decades, of careful crafting and execution. There is no reason why this work cannot start now in at least some measure.

Many complain that the primary failure of Fannie and Freddie lay in its ownership structure: heads I win, tails you lose; or, in other words, the privatization of profits (for the shareholders and executives) in good times but the socialization of downside risk (for the taxpayer). Having been delisted from New York Stock Exchange and being in conservatorship, Fannie and Freddie are effectively nationalized at the current point in time.

Simply nationalizing them for the indefinite future, however, will not fix the state of mortgage finance in the United States. The collapse of Fannie and Freddie during the financial crisis of 2008 is in fact emblematic of a much broader and worldwide problem with government-owned enterprises. The German *Landesbanken*, guaranteed by the state and explicitly public entities (unlike Fannie and Freddie), also went all-in in funding the real estate boom in the United States and the United Kingdom, only to be the first banks to fail and be bailed out in the crisis. The Spanish *Cajas*, similar to the savings and loan associations in the United States, funded the biggest construction boom in Spain and are now deemed an important contributor to its economic malaise. Fannie and Freddie are the poster children of government-related institutions, often set up with an initially limited and worthwhile mandate but grown far beyond their initial purpose into uncontrollable and systemically risky behemoths.

Hence, nothing short of bringing the shutter down on Fannie and Freddie in the long run will suffice. As we were completing this book in August of 2010, the Obama administration has promised to lay out its proposals to reform these institutions by early 2011. This book presents and analyzes several proposals, including our own.

First and foremost, government entities of the scale of Fannie and Freddie should simply not exist. That is, their job should be performed by private markets or not at all. However, if these entities must exist, then they should be run in smaller sizes as "boring public utilities" with three features:

1. They should face highly ring-fenced usage of government guarantees—in other words, they can't run a casino with taxpayer money.
2. The guarantees should be explicitly recognized on the federal balance sheet so that there is no Ponzi scheme of each presidential administration's passing the risk down to the next one. This would ensure that the scale of government entities is a function of preallocated fiscal budgets.

3. The sole purpose of these entities should be to remedy a clearly identified market failure or, in other words, to fill in where markets do not exist or are unlikely to achieve socially efficient outcomes. This purpose should be achieved through public-private partnerships, allowing private markets to grow side by side. Thereby, the government entities would pave the way for their own graceful exit in a prespecified period from the time of their birth.

More concretely, one of our novel proposals attempts to balance the short-term transition and long-term efficiency issues in moving away from the GSEs. We propose that the GSEs' investment function—which allowed them to invest in mortgage-backed securities as hedge funds or proprietary-trading desks—should be closed and wound down in an orderly, gradual fashion. Since the early 1990s, asset management firms have become an important part of capital markets and can pick up the slack in the secondary mortgage-backed security market. The government has no business running a gigantic hedge fund.

Because mortgage default guarantees have been an essential element of the development and liquidity of the core of the mortgage markets in the United States, mortgage default insurance should be preserved in some form, but the role of the GSEs therein should be substantially reduced. Arguably, the private sector cannot be the sole provider, as this insurance is systemic owing to its dependence on macroeconomic events. When a private insurance firm fails to honor its insurance, other firms will likely be in the same situation and thus be unable to reinsure. Yet because of the lack of adequate governance, incentive structures, and accountability (let alone political considerations), the public sector alone cannot step into the breach either.

We recommend a pragmatic middle ground: a public-private partnership in which the private sector decides which mortgage guarantees to provide and prices the guarantees but insures (say) only a 25% fraction of each of these mortgages, while the government is a silent partner, insuring the remaining 75% and receiving the corresponding insurance premiums. The private-sector firms (which could even be a cooperative of several financial firms) would need to be well regulated—in particular, well capitalized for the extent of systemic risk they take on and subject to an irrefutable resolution authority. Further, the partnership model of guarantees should cover only the plain vanilla "conforming" mortgages with strict underwriting criteria (such as maximum 80% loan-to-value ratios). The provision of default insurance to non-vanilla mortgages should be left entirely to well-capitalized private firms.

Many other developed countries' mortgage markets function without mortgage guarantees. Yet their secondary mortgage markets tend to be less developed: banks hold on to a larger fraction of loans, and long-term fixed-rate mortgage products are less prevalent than in the United States. Preserving the central role of the 30-year fixed-rate mortgage requires a well-functioning securitization channel. Moreover, these alternative mortgage market architectures proved just as fragile in the financial crisis, resulting in large-scale bank bailouts, not dissimilar to the GSE bailout.

Finally, the desirability of the public mission of funding home ownership is debatable. The United States has more programs subsidizing home ownership than any other developed country, yet (and, arguably, therefore) its housing bust was worse than almost anywhere else. These programs have ultimately failed to deliver higher home ownership or housing affordability relative to conditions in other countries that have experienced less government interference in housing markets. Fundamentally, these subsidies distort the relative price of housing and lead to overinvestment and overconsumption of housing, ultimately subtracting from economic growth.

Regardless of which position one takes in the debate about encouraging home ownership, it seems clear that the GSEs' way of subsidizing home ownership through unfunded government guarantees is not an effective approach. Academic research has cast serious doubts on the ability of the GSE guarantees to help low-income households, arguing that they have mostly lowered mortgage payments for the rich. To the extent that housing subsidy programs must exist, we believe that they should be on a much smaller scale and are better housed in the Federal Housing Administration (FHA) and/or some other agency within the Department of Housing and Urban Development (HUD). This would make their costs explicitly an on-balance-sheet fiscal item for the federal government, providing transparency to the taxpayer. Any future architecture of housing finance in America should contemplate that more housing credit and construction are *not* the answer to the current-day economic challenges.

Of course, fixing and unwinding Fannie and Freddie will not be enough if they are simply replaced by other government-sponsored enterprises. The spirit of our reform proposals concerns all government-sponsored enterprises. We even suggest limits on unfunded Federal Reserve interventions in markets and provide a broadly applicable blueprint of how to organize publicly financed utilities, keep their excesses in check, and always have reasonable exit strategies.

Likewise, fixing and unwinding Fannie and Freddie will not be enough if they are simply replaced by other systemically risky private-sector institutions that are ultimately too big or too interconnected to fail. Any redesign of the mortgage market must enforce competition in mortgage originations and securitization and proper capital requirements for all firms involved. If mortgage guarantees that are provided by private firms largely remain as off-balance-sheet or unfunded items, then these firms would be the Fannie and the Freddie of the future but in a new guise, and we can be sure that their risks in the end would be borne by the taxpayer.

One argument against doing anything radical to change the GSEs—or at least against doing anything soon—is the perception that the private sector has abandoned the mortgage market. As of the first half of 2010, Fannie and Freddie plus the FHA were buying or guaranteeing more than 90% of all residential mortgages that were originated. However, what we may be observing is the mortgage version of "Catch 22." When the mortgage securitization market dried up in late 2007, after the revelations of all of the "private-label" subprime related securities that had gone south, the federal government naturally pushed Fannie and Freddie and the FHA forward to fill the gap—including a near doubling of the size of mortgages (in some parts of the United States) that would qualify for their support. Now that they are heavily entrenched in a much wider swath of the mortgage market, their government backing means that they have lower costs and are thus subsidizing mortgages. This makes it difficult, or perhaps impossible, for private-label securitization to be reestablished.

Accordingly, the heavy presence of Fannie and Freddie and the FHA currently may be indicative not of the private sector's disinterest in reviving private-label securitization but simply of the private sector's inability to compete against the subsidies, which crowd out the competition. This conundrum, too, calls for the radical restructuring of Fannie and Freddie that we advocate in this book.

1

FEEDING THE BEAST

The GSEs play an extraordinarily successful double game . . . [telling] Congress and the news media, "Don't worry, the government is not on the hook"—and then turn around and tell Wall Street, "Don't worry, the government really is on the hook."

—*Richard Carnell (Fordham University Law Professor and former Assistant Secretary of the Treasury), Senate testimony, February 10, 2004*

In 1818, a nineteen-year-old English girl, Mary Shelley, published her first novel. The novel tells the story of a young, talented scientist who discovers how to create life from the inanimate. Collecting old human bones and tissue, the scientist constructs a man from scratch and brings him to life, only to be disgusted by his appearance and shape, calling him the Monster. The scientist deserts the monster, and, left to its own devices, his creation causes havoc and mayhem. In the finale of the story, as the scientist confronts the monster, the monster eventually destroys its creator and, stricken with grief, takes its own life. Shelley decided that the name of the talented scientist should be the title for the novel: *Frankenstein*.

Former executives of Fannie and Freddie, members of Congress, and past administration officials all talk about the good work of the government-sponsored enterprises (GSEs) Fannie Mae and Freddie Mac; and, they will add, if it were not for the equivalent of an economic asteroid hitting the markets, all would be fine. They will point to affordable housing goals and the benefits to the underprivileged.

We are skeptics.

If the government was Doctor Frankenstein, surely the GSEs were its monster. Born of a well-intentioned and economically efficient goal of creating liquidity in the secondary mortgage market, these institutions morphed into typical profit-taking firms with an important exception—the government served as the backstop for the majority of their risks. While the government subsidies went primarily to CEOs, shareholders, and wealthier homeowners, the costs were borne by society as a whole. As of 1970, when Fannie Mae had been recently privatized and

Freddie Mac was newly created, they represented 4.4% of the mortgage market; by 1991, they captured 28.4%; by the time of the financial crisis, they held 41.3%, with a combined $1.43 trillion mortgage portfolio and $3.50 trillion in mortgage-backed security (MBS) guarantees; and, as of August 2010, they had left the U.S. taxpayers with a hit of close to $150 billion, with some projections anticipating that this figure will more than double in years to come, with substantial downside risk.

We start by describing what the GSEs do—what roles they play in the mortgage markets. We then trace the origins of Fannie Mae and Freddie Mac, what special features of these enterprises caused the financial markets to treat them specially, and what allowed them to register their staggering growth.

1.1 THE ESSENCE OF THE GSES

What exactly do Fannie and Freddie do? The GSEs are engaged in two somewhat related businesses: residential mortgage securitization (currently about $3.5 trillion) and residential mortgage investment (currently about $1.7 trillion).

In the securitization business, the GSEs buy mortgages from originators (mostly fixed-rate, single-family home mortgages, although they also buy some adjustable-rate mortgages and some mortgages in the multifamily market); they form pools of these mortgages (so that the "law of large numbers" reduces the variability in outcomes that might arise from a single mortgage); and they issue (sell) "pass-through" mortgage-backed securities that are formed from these pools to investors. These MBS represent claims on the interest and principal repayments that are "passed through" from the pool of mortgage borrowers to the securities investors (minus various fees).[1]

Because the investors have no direct knowledge of the creditworthiness of the mortgage borrower, they need to be reassured that they will receive the promised interest and principal repayments. Both Fannie Mae and Freddie Mac provide guarantees to investors in their MBS against the risk of default by borrowers of the underlying mortgages. In return, both charge a "guarantee fee."

Although the GSE guarantee (so long as it can be honored) removes the credit risk from the securities, the MBS investor is still subject to interest rate risk. Any long-lived fixed-rate debt instrument carries interest rate risk. When interest rates for new securities are higher than the interest rate on an existing (but otherwise comparable) security, the value of the latter decreases; when interest rates for new securities are lower, the value of the existing security increases. However, for fixed-rate mortgages (and the MBS that are formed from them), the interest rate risk for the investor is heightened, because mortgage borrowers are usually able to prepay their mortgage (and, in the United States, do so without paying any fee or penalty).[2]

The second business for the GSEs is mortgage investment. They buy and hold residential mortgages (or, more often, their own MBS). The funding for these investments comes overwhelmingly from issuing debt. They earn net income on the "spread": the difference between the interest yield on the mortgages that they hold and the interest rate on the debt that they have issued. Because their debt is implicitly guaranteed by the U.S. government, GSE debt is relatively risk insensitive. Further, the GSE shareholders do not pay a premium for these government guarantees or bear the full cost of their failure. Hence, from the GSEs' standpoint, the cost of issuing debt is less than the costs of issuing equity, and they have a strong incentive to try to leverage themselves as much as possible—to issue as much debt and as little equity—to the extent that their creditors and regulators will permit.[3] By owning these on-balance-sheet mortgages, the GSEs are exposed to interest rate risk as well as credit risk.

The timeline in the appendix lays out the key reforms and events punctuating the evolution of U.S. housing finance policy from its inception in the 1930s all the way to the current state of affairs. There have been three somewhat distinct phases: the early phase, in the Depression era, helps us to understand how and why the federal government established a foothold in mortgage finance; the privatization phase, starting in the late 1960s, paved the way for the GSEs' expansion on the back of government guarantees; and the debt phase, starting in 1992, mandated the GSEs to serve "mission" goals while simultaneously being accorded highly favorable regulatory treatment with regard to their leverage. The end result is the present debacle of Fannie Mae, Freddie Mac, and U.S. housing finance.

1.2 BEGINNINGS

The origins of Fannie Mae and Freddie Mac go back to the era of the Great Depression. The stock market crash of 1929–33, and the failures of more than 8,000 commercial banks, as well as thousands of savings and loan (S&L) institutions (which are frequently described as "thrifts") inflicted widespread economic misery across the United States.

Among the victims of this trauma was the residential mortgage lending system. Before the mid-1930s, the standard mortgage loan had a five-year term, with interim interest payments and a required balloon payment for the full amount at the end of five years. The expectation was that the mortgage would be refinanced at that time. Banks and S&Ls were the primary originators and holders of mortgages, although life insurance companies also were significant holders of mortgages (especially of multifamily mortgages). The economic implosion of the early 1930s, however, meant that many lenders were unwilling to refinance, and many borrowers could not repay. Home foreclosures were widespread; and the losses on the foreclosed loans contributed to the failures of thousands of banks and S&Ls.

The first piece of legislation that made any effort to address these issues preceded the Roosevelt administration's "New Deal." In 1932, during the final year of the Hoover administration, the Congress created the Federal Home Loan Bank System: 12 regional Federal Home Loan Banks (FHLBs) that were owned by the S&L institutions and a few life insurance companies in the regional territories of the FHLBs and that were regulated by a new federal agency: the Federal Home Loan Bank Board (which would soon also be the national regulator of S&Ls). The FHLB System could borrow funds in the capital markets, and the individual FHLBs could turn around and lend the funds to their member-owners, who were the primary originators of mortgages at the time. Because the FHLB System was a creation of the federal government, it could borrow at favorable rates, and the FHLBs could pass those favorable rates on to their member-owners.

In an important sense, the FHLB System was an early "government-sponsored enterprise" (although that term was not used until decades later). It reflected for the first time what was to become a distinguishing feature of the U.S. housing finance for next eight decades: borrowing in the name of the government (explicitly or implicitly) to promote household borrowing in the form of mortgages.

With the New Deal came a flurry of legislation that affected the financial system, with some of the legislation leaving a lasting impact on residential mortgage finance. This included the creation of the Federal Housing Administration (FHA) in 1934 to offer mortgage insurance to lenders on qualified mortgages and of the Federal National Mortgage Association (FNMA) in 1938 to purchase FHA-insured mortgages. Funding for these purchases came through the FHA's issuance of bonds in the capital markets. The FNMA subsequently acquired the nickname "Fannie Mae" from the bond traders who dealt in those bonds, and the nickname stuck.

Over the next two decades, Fannie Mae's scope was expanded. First, it gained the authority to buy the mortgages insured by the Veterans Administration (VA), another creation of the Congress, the powers of which included the guaranteeing of qualifying mortgages—in this case, the mortgages of veterans. Then, Fannie Mae's status as a government agency was confirmed, and it was made exempt from state and local income taxes, which was (and is) a substantial competitive advantage relative to private financial firms. As another advantage, the Federal Reserve Banks were required to perform various services for Fannie Mae. And Fannie Mae was to provide "special assistance" for certain kinds of mortgages, a precursor to the "mission" regulation of the GSEs in the 1990s and 2000s. The debt that Fannie Mae issued came to be known as "agency" debt, or just as "Agencies" (a label that persisted through the subsequent morphing of Fannie Mae, and which has applied to Freddie Mac's debt as well).

Through these steps, the government's foothold in mortgage finance was born.

From its chartering in 1938 through the middle of the 1960s, Fannie Mae was a relatively minor presence in the overall residential market—more symbolic than substantive. The major institutional holders of residential mortgages during this period were S&Ls, commercial banks, and life insurance companies. Somewhat paradoxically, Fannie Mae grew the most on the back of the U.S. government only when the government began to "disown" it, though never fully.

1.3 PRIVATIZATION OF THE GSES

By far, the most important legislation affecting Fannie Mae was its conversion into a private company in 1968. It was primarily for accounting purposes. The Johnson administration wanted Fannie Mae privatized, so as to remove its debt from the federal government's books, thereby reducing the size of the national debt. In addition, a change in federal budgeting procedures at the time would have counted Fannie Mae's net purchases of mortgages as current government expenditures, which would have meant that those net purchases would have added to recorded federal budget deficits—something that any presidential administration would want to avoid doing during its own term.

The privatization meant that Fannie Mae was spun off to the private sector and became a publicly traded company, with its shares listed on the New York Stock Exchange (NYSE). However, Fannie Mae retained its federal charter and the special status and privileges that went with it. Fannie Mae also had its own special regulator: the Department of Housing and Urban Development (HUD), which had been created as a cabinet-level department in 1965 and retained some regulatory powers over Fannie Mae. Another prominent indicator of the specialness of Fannie Mae, despite its apparent structure as just another private (publicly traded) company, was the power of the president of the United States to appoint five board members to the Fannie Mae board of directors. No other company that was listed on the NYSE had presidential appointees on its board.

Simultaneously with the spinning off of Fannie Mae into the private sector, the same 1968 legislation created the Government National Mortgage Association (GNMA, which was subsequently dubbed "Ginnie Mae") within HUD as an agency that would securitize FHA- and VA-insured mortgages. And next to arrive on the scene was Freddie Mac in 1970. Ownership of Freddie Mac was placed with the Federal Home Loan Bank System, which was owned by the S&L industry.[4] The three board members of the Federal Home Loan Bank Board became the board members and de facto regulators of Freddie Mac. (Shares of Freddie Mac would be made available to the general public almost two decades later.) Freddie Mac was expected to buy mortgage loans from the S&L industry and securitize them, although it was not restricted from buying mortgage loans from other originators. Because Freddie Mac (like Fannie Mae) was the creature of Congress, it too was a GSE.

Fannie Mae, too, received authorization to expand its mortgage purchases to encompass mortgages that were not insured by FHA or VA. However, both Fannie Mae and Freddie Mac were restricted (by HUD and the Bank Board, respectively) in the size of mortgage loan that they could purchase, either for securitization or for holding in their portfolios. This maximum loan size came to be known as the "conforming loan" limit. Mortgages that exceeded the conforming limit came to be known as "jumbos." From 1975 to 1977, for example, the conforming loan limit was $55,000; from 1977 to 1979 the conforming loan limit was $75,000. In 1980 the limit was raised to $93,750 and was subsequently linked to an index of housing prices. For comparison purposes, the median price of the sale of an existing house was $35,300 in 1975 and was $62,200 in 1980; the median price of a new house was $39,300 and $64,600 in those two years, respectively. Thus, the conforming loan limit was substantially above median prices, whether measured by sales of existing homes or new homes; this pattern has continued to prevail to the present day, explaining the reach of the GSEs in affecting housing finance of a substantial proportion of the U.S. households.

What is not commonly known is the financial difficulty that was experienced by Fannie Mae in the early 1980s. Like the savings and loan industry that it resembled (because, like the S&L industry, it was borrowing from the public and holding fixed-rate mortgages in its portfolio), Fannie Mae was squeezed by the high interest rates of the late 1970s and early 1980s. Holding a portfolio of long-lived fixed-rate mortgages that had been originated at lower interest rates than were prevailing in the early 1980s, it ran net losses in the early 1980s. Although Fannie Mae remained solvent on a book-value basis, there was widespread recognition that it was insolvent on a market-value basis. It survived the experience, however, and lower interest rates after 1982 eventually provided financial relief.

The savings and loan industry was not so fortunate. It was a preview of the financial storm that would crush the financial system some 25 years later. The interest rate squeeze and a poorly structured deregulation of the industry in the early 1980s led to rapid growth in nontraditional investments in the mid-1980s and the eventual insolvencies of hundreds of S&Ls by the late 1980s and early 1990s. The federal government, through yet another agency (the Federal Savings and Loan Insurance Corporation, or the FSLIC), was guaranteeing the deposit liabilities of the insolvent S&Ls. Hence, as in the financial crisis of 2007–9, it was the federal government that bore the net losses of these insolvencies. The bill at the time came to about $150 billion.

In response to the interest rate squeeze of the late 1970s and early 1980s, the President's Commission on Housing issued a report on April 29, 1982, calling for greater deregulation of mortgage banking and an increased role for capital markets in the secondary market for mortgages. It had been just over a decade earlier in 1970 and 1971, respectively, that Ginnie Mae and Freddie Mac had first issued MBS; Fannie Mae had issued its first MBS in 1981. Together, these GSEs had given birth to the U.S. mortgage securitization market. The dizzying heights that this securitization market eventually scaled played a central role in the financial crisis of 2007–9. However, in 1982 this market was a fledgling one. It was widely noted that the secondary market for mortgages was so illiquid that financial firms were stuck holding mortgage loans, creating huge dislocations as conditions worsened.

As such, the idea behind MBS was financial innovation at its best: the banking sector did not have enough capital (or risk appetite) to hold all of the mortgage loans, yet these individual loans were too illiquid to be sold easily to investors. By pooling the loans into MBS and selling the MBS to investors in the capital market at large—including pension funds, insurance companies, and the emerging mutual fund sector—the mortgage market would become much more liquid. This would simultaneously allow this market to expand and improve mortgage loan pricing, resulting in lower mortgage interest rates for homeowners.

It was not until the early 1980s that the Wall Street firm Salomon Brothers created a mortgage trading operation. With this operation, the firm created and tapped into a new class of interested investors that focused on the MBS market. The operation, run by Lewis Ranieri and made famous (some would argue infamous) in Michael Lewis's book *Liar's Poker*, just needed a kick-start, and the deregulation of mortgage finance took off. Ironically, one of the conclusions of the commission was that this deregulation would put an end to the government-sponsored enterprises (GSEs) such as Fannie Mae and Freddie Mac: "Eventually, the Commission believes, both FNMA [Fannie Mae] and FHLMC [Freddie Mac] should become entirely private corporations, without special access to the deep pockets of the Treasury."

The commission was just a *tad* off in its prediction. At the end of 1981, when the commission was starting its work, Fannie and Freddie represented just 7.1% of the residential mortgage market and held $64.8 billion worth of mortgages in their portfolios and guaranteed an additional $20.6 billion. A decade later, their market share had grown to an extraordinary 28.4%, with corresponding portfolio holdings of $153.4 billion and guarantees of $714.5 billion. By 2002, they held $1.21 trillion and guaranteed $1.52 trillion, equivalent to a 44.7% share of the residential mortgage market. This growth of Fannie and Freddie is depicted in figure 1.1. The left-hand side provides the total dollar value of Fannie's and Freddie's commitments to the mortgage market through their portfolios and their net MBS issuances, while the right-hand side represents their overall share of the mortgage market.

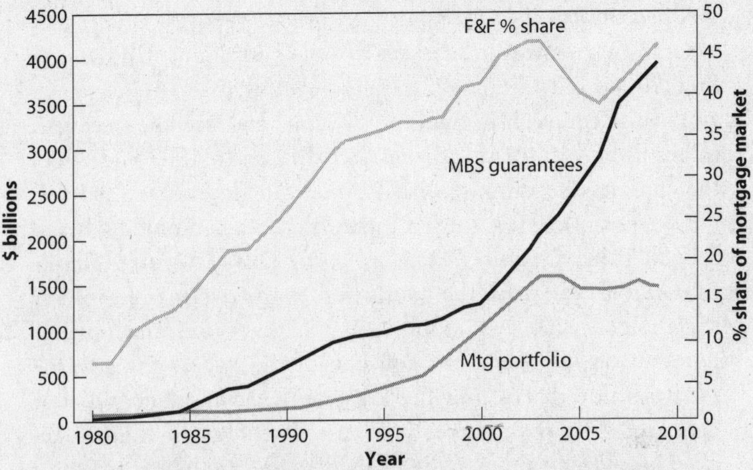

Figure 1.1: Growth of the GSEs from 1980 until 2009. Source: Federal Housing Finance Agency and Federal Reserve

How did the commission get its prediction so wrong? When mortgage markets were deregulated, Fannie and Freddie were not meant to be the winners. The Reagan administration at the time thought the opposite. It argued that deregulation—the act of lessening government's control in favor of a free market—would lead to a race to the top as private-sector firms would enter the sector and compete openly. Free markets generally work well, with capital flowing to its most efficient use, ending up with better-run firms. So the theory goes.

But there was nothing free about these markets. As we have already highlighted, Fannie and Freddie had a special status, which meant that the financial markets believed that there were implicit government guarantees on any debt that they issued and on the mortgage guarantees that they provided. No firm could compete with Fannie and Freddie under these circumstances: they paid less taxes, could borrow at cheaper rates, and were lightly regulated in that they faced low capital requirements for holding similar risks compared to private-sector counterparts. Opening up mortgage markets without restraining Fannie and Freddie was like bringing a knife to a gun fight.

It is, of course, intriguing how Fannie and Freddie managed to get away with it for decade after decade. In 1999 and 2000, the conservative think tank, the American Enterprise Institute, ran a series of conferences on these firms, the end product being a book titled *Serving Two Masters, Yet Out of Control: Fannie Mae and Freddie Mac*. The book refers to the two masters—their shareholders and their public mission of encouraging greater home ownership—and the collision of the two as the government subsidy that is provided for one (i.e., the public mission) gets exploited by the other (i.e., the shareholders). The conference brought together individuals of quite different ideologies who reached similar conclusions.

One fascinating piece was written by Ralph Nader, the consumer advocate, political activist, and left-wing ideologue, who outlines in detail the interconnections between successive presidential administrations and the payroll of Fannie and Freddie, documenting the heavy (and aggressive) lobbying by these firms:

> Fannie Mae and Freddie Mac are fast learners. Born of the federal bureaucracy, these enterprises have swiftly and skillfully managed to pick up the roughshod tactics of the private corporate world and at the same time cling tightly to one of the federal government's deepest and most lucrative welfare troughs. . . . The combination has produced two GSEs that are not only too big to be allowed to fail but perhaps too influential and too politically connected to be regulated or shaped effectively in the public interest. Any suggestion that their power be limited or that subsidies be reduced triggers an immediate no-holds-barred counterattack from Fannie and Freddie. As John Buckley, Fannie Mae's vice president for communications, bluntly told the *Wall Street Journal*, "We're not casual about managing our political risk."[5]

Some members of Congress and the leadership at the GSEs' regulator did attempt to rein in the GSEs, but the inadequate numbers of the former and the inadequate regulatory powers of the latter hindered these efforts—a condition that the GSEs lobbied strenuously to perpetuate. In response to a 2004 congressional bill that was aimed at enhanced regulation of Fannie and Freddie, for example, Fannie, with remarkable bravado, ran a television advertisement the day before the Senate Banking Committee was to work on the bill.[6] The advertisement shows a concerned Hispanic man. He says "Uh-oh," and the wife responds, "What?" "It looks like Congress is talking about new regulations for Fannie Mae," the man states. "Will that keep us from getting that lower mortgage rate?" the women replies. "Some economists say rates may go up," he says. "But that could mean we won't be able to afford the new house," says the woman. "I know," the husband concludes.

Fannie Mae—created and supported by the government—was now going after the government head-on. The monster was destroying its Frankenstein creator. Needless to say, the bill died.

While Nader's article makes clear how difficult it was for Washington to put constraints on Fannie Mae and Freddie Mac, the question remains, How did they grow so big?

1.4 DROWNING IN DEBT

With the deregulation of the mortgage finance market, the decade of the 1980s was a period of substantial growth for Fannie and Freddie. At the end of the decade, Fannie and Freddie were fundamentally entrenched as parallel GSEs, with similar structures, privileges, responsibilities, and limitations. The last major legislation to impact the GSEs until the financial crisis of 2007–9 was the Federal Housing Enterprises Financial Safety and Soundness Act (FHEFSSA) of 1992. It produced a number of important rules, one in particular related to capital requirements.

In particular, a risk-based capital regulatory regime was specified for Fannie and Freddie and their two main functions: securitizing and guaranteeing the credit risk of MBS, and investing in MBS or other similar portfolios of mortgages. With respect to the first function, the capital buffer that the GSEs were required to hold against these guarantees was 0.45% (i.e., $.45 per $100.00 of guaranteed mortgages), which implied that the Congress believed that residential mortgages were quite safe instruments to guarantee against credit risk—or that the Congress meant to subsidize these guarantees and was (if push came to shove) prepared to cover any losses. With respect to the second function, the GSEs were to hold 2.50% capital against their balance sheet assets (of which mortgages are by far the largest category). Thus, for every $100 in mortgages held, they could (in principle) fund those mortgages with $97.50 in debt and only $2.50 in equity.

In comparison to any other financial institution, Fannie and Freddie were afforded extraordinarily light capital requirements.

For example, the capital requirement for federally insured banks and thrifts to hold residential mortgages was substantially greater: 4%. As a result, Fannie and Freddie had much higher leverage ratios—total assets to shareholder equity—than did comparable banking institutions.

To many fixed-income practitioners and analysts, the GSEs' growth and the expansion of securitization markets for mortgage finance should be considered a success story. But there was a darker side to the interaction between the GSEs and the banking sector: while banks were charged a 4% capital requirement for holding a portfolio of mortgage loans, they were charged only 40% of this, or 1.60%, if they held GSE MBS instead. Within the financial sector, this creates perverse incentives for banks to load up on GSE MBS, thereby increasing leverage all the way around the sector.

To see this, note that if a bank originated $100 worth of mortgage loans, it would have to hold a minimum $4.00 of capital to be considered adequately capitalized. If the bank sold these loans to the GSEs and the GSEs securitized them into MBS, however, it could buy back the GSE MBS and hold only $1.60 in capital, even though its portfolio holdings would be identical. Because the GSEs are required to hold only $.45, this means that, for the same level of risk, the capital requirement for the financial sector as a whole now is just $2.05, or 51% of what it used to be. There is little doubt that the growth in securitization is related to this type of regulatory arbitrage.

In terms of data to support this point, consider the first year of the crisis in 2007. According to *Inside Mortgage Finance*, of the $5.2 trillion in MBS guarantees by Fannie Mae, Freddie Mac, and Ginnie Mae, approximately 37% was held by the banking sector—$817 billion by commercial banks, $790 billion by Fannie and Freddie themselves, $257 billion by thrifts, and $91 billion by the FHLBs. And just six firms—Bank of America, Wachovia, JP Morgan Chase, Citigroup, and Wells Fargo—contributed 48% to the commercial bank holdings, and just three thrifts—ING Bank, Washington Mutual, and Hudson City Savings—40% to the thrift portfolios. This is substantive evidence against capital markets' holding the credit risk—that is, the "originate-to-distribute" mode—and much more support for banks' taking on the risk, albeit as a counterparty to the highly levered GSEs.

To document the leverage of the GSEs, figure 1.2 graphs the ratio of total assets on the balance sheet divided by the shareholder equity of the combined Fannie and Freddie (gray line). The figure takes as a starting point the date of the 1992 legislation that set the capital requirements and continues the ratio until the end of 2007. (Of course, by the end of 2008, shareholder equity had gone negative, and the GSEs were taken into conservatorship.) Over this period, the GSE leverage ratios generally ranged between values of 20 to 40 whereas the commercial banking sector had ratios of 10 to 15. The only match to emerge for GSE leverage was in the form of investment banks, especially during 2003–7—a competitive race to the bottom that we will explore in detail in chapter 3.

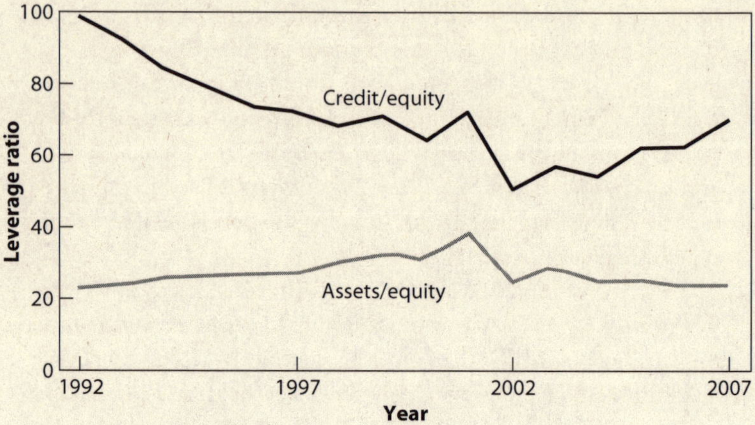

Figure 1.2: Leverage Ratios of GSEs. Source: Federal Housing Finance Agency

However, these ratios do not tell the entire story. As shown by figure 1.1, most of the credit risk of GSEs is in the form of guarantees of defaults on mortgages sold to MBS investors. These guarantees do not appear on the balance sheet of the GSEs. As a useful exercise, the black line in figure 1.2 sums up all of the credit risk that is contained in both their mortgage portfolios and their credit guarantees of MBS (i.e., the "credit" numerator is the sum of their on-balance-sheet assets plus their outstanding MBS). This is roughly equivalent to what the banking sector does when it holds "whole loan" mortgages (i.e., the mortgages themselves, and not MBS) and hedges the interest rate risk in those mortgages.

The numbers are simply startling. The credit-based leverage ratios now range between levels of 50 to 100 over the period.[7] Even more troublesome was the GSEs' behavior from 2002 onward. As regulators became more aware of the mere size of the GSEs, coupled with accounting scandals in 2003 and 2004, there was a general recognition that their size and leverage had to be curtailed. And, in fact, there was some apparent success. From the end of 2001 to 2007, the "official" leverage ratio dropped from

38 to 23 and the portfolio stopped growing. But the credit-based leverage ratio that also included the off-balance-sheet guarantees—the total credit risk divided by shareholder equity as shown in figure 1.2—barely budged from 72 to 69. As figure 1.1 shows, the GSEs had simply replaced growth in their mortgage portfolios with growth in guarantees of MBS.

1.5 ONE BIG FAT SUBSIDY

The mortgage credit risk of Fannie Mae and Freddie Mac combined grew at an astonishing 16% (11%) annual growth rate from 1980 (1992) through 2007. We saw that this growth was financed using borrowed money and levels of leverage far in excess of other financial institutions. Why would debt investors finance such growth?

Because of the special status and treatment of the GSEs that were described earlier in this chapter, the financial markets have historically treated them specially: the financial markets believed (correctly, as it turned out, or as a self-fulfilling prophesy) that if either company ever experienced financial difficulties, the federal government would likely intercede to make sure that the company's creditors did not suffer any losses. This belief persisted despite the explicit statement on all GSE securities that these securities were not full-faith-and-credit obligations of the U.S. government. The belief seems largely rational given that for most practical purposes, GSE debt is on par with Treasuries as "liquidity" or "risk-free securities" and therefore is held in hoards by financial firms just as Treasuries are (in fact, 50% of GSE debt was held by financial firms in 2008). The "halo" effect of all of the special features of the GSEs was just too strong for them not to be deemed as too big to fail.

With an implicit guarantee on their debt, Fannie and Freddie were able to borrow at interest rates that were below what the financial markets otherwise would have demanded. This meant that it was quite profitable for the GSEs to purchase mortgages and offer credit default guarantees below fundamental rates, allowing them to vanquish any competition and grow unfettered. Because fixed-income investors—either those holding Fannie and Freddie debt or MBS guaranteed by Fannie and Freddie—believed that there was a government backstop, market discipline went out the window, and there was no one left to restrain Fannie and Freddie.

As described in the preceding section, adding to this subsidy was the fact that Fannie and Freddie had much lower capital requirements than did commercial banks and investment banks, for guaranteeing as well as holding MBS. With such a lack of a level playing field, there was really no free market. Instead of capital flowing to its most efficient use, as the deregulation of mortgage markets in the 1980s had anticipated, capital was in fact flowing to its most *levered* use. There was no one left to restrain Fannie and Freddie, of course, other than the federal government; but in the pursuit of myopic goals of boosting home ownership at all costs, each successive presidential administration turned a blind eye.

In a seminal study in 1996, the Congressional Budget Office (CBO) provided an estimate of the government subsidy for Fannie and Freddie in 1995. The two main factors that went into their analysis were the reduced cost of financing compared to other highly rated financial institutions (e.g., 0.70% per year lower interest rate), and the lower cost of issuing MBS (e.g., 0.40%). Their estimated annual total subsidy was $6.9 billion, a very large number fifteen years ago. Moreover, the CBO argued that at least one-third was a complete transfer of wealth from the government to shareholders; that is, only two-thirds trickled down to the mortgage market.

At the time that the study was announced, Fannie and Freddie went into attack mode and criticized the methodology and results. When one looks at the CBO's assumptions, however, one could provide an argument the other way: the CBO underestimated the subsidy. The main assumption was that, without government support, Fannie and Freddie would have had the same amount of debt and off-balance-sheet guarantees. But their leverage was extraordinary and almost certainly would have commanded a much lower credit rating. Further, no adjustment was made for the added systemic risk that was produced—the steady, unfettered rise of housing-related debt in the United States as part of national wealth—and retained by Fannie and Freddie.

In a May 2001 updated study, the CBO estimated that the annual implicit subsidy had risen to $13.6 billion by the year 2000. A few years later, Federal Reserve Board economist Wayne Passmore, using a similar methodology and a standard discounted earnings model over a forward-looking 25-year horizon, estimated that the aggregate value of the subsidy ranged somewhere between $119 billion and $164 billion, of which shareholders received respectively between $50 and $97 billion. Astonishingly, the subsidy was almost equal to the market value of these two GSEs, providing further evidence against the desirability of their existence in their current form.[8]

Year after year, a large number of economists and policy makers questioned the distortions that were being created by this "big fat" subsidy. In what is perhaps one of the more eloquent summaries of subsidy-related distortions, a speech on May 19, 2005, by Federal Reserve Chairman Alan Greenspan explains the growth of GSE balance sheets and their guarantee-driven shareholder value:[9]

> Although prospectuses for GSE debt are required by law to stipulate that such instruments are not backed by the full faith and credit of the U.S. government, investors worldwide have concluded that our government will not allow GSEs to default. . . . Investors have provided Fannie and Freddie with a powerful vehicle for achieving profits that are virtually guaranteed through the rapid growth of their balance sheets, and the resultant scale has given them an advantage that their potential private-sector competitors cannot meet. As a result, their annual return on equity, which has often exceeded 30 percent, is far in excess of

the average annual return of approximately 15 percent that has been earned by other large financial competitors holding substantially similar assets. Virtually none of the GSE excess return reflects higher yields on assets; it is almost wholly attributable to subsidized borrowing costs. . . . The Federal Reserve Board has been unable to find any credible purpose for the huge balance sheets built by Fannie and Freddie other than the creation of profit through the exploitation of the market-granted subsidy.

2

TICKING TIME BOMB

"We didn't really know what we were buying," said Marc Gott, a former director in Fannie's loan servicing department. "This system was designed for plain vanilla loans, and we were trying to push chocolate sundaes through the gears."

—*Charles Duhigg,* New York Times, *October 5, 2008*

On October 28, 1992, President George H. W. Bush signed into law H.R. 5334, The Housing and Community Development Act of 1992. As described in chapter 1, Title XIII of the law, the Federal Housing Enterprises Financial Safety and Soundness Act (FHEFSSA), created rules for the two largest government-sponsored enterprises (GSEs), Fannie Mae and Freddie Mac. In his remarks, President Bush said:

> This legislation addresses the problems created by the rapid expansion of certain GSEs in the last decade. It establishes a means to protect taxpayers from the possible risks posed by GSEs in housing finance. The bill creates a regulator within the Department of Housing and Urban Development (HUD) to ensure that the housing GSEs are adequately capitalized and operated safely. . . . I regret,

> however, that the Congress chose to attach these important reforms to a housing bill that contains numerous provisions that raise serious concerns. My Administration worked diligently to craft a compromise housing bill that would target assistance where it is needed most, expand home ownership opportunities, ensure fiscal integrity, and empower recipients of Federal housing assistance.

Title XIII was a compromise between those politicians who wished to restrain the GSEs and those who wanted to unleash them. It turned out not to be a very fair fight.

On the one hand, FHEFSSA created a separate prudential (safety and soundness) regulator for Fannie Mae and Freddie Mac: the Office of Federal Housing Enterprise Oversight (OFHEO), which was lodged in HUD. It was clear to many observers at the time, however, that a policy-oriented department such as HUD was not the appropriate agency for lodging a prudential regulator. While there may have been a policy angle in this being allowed, it should also be noted that Fannie and Freddie spent more than $200 million lobbying the Congress to avoid tighter oversight. The GSEs were essentially a government-supported banking system and should have been regulated as such.

On the other hand, FHEFSSA specified a set of "mission goals": essentially, efforts to help support housing for low- and moderate-income households, as well as a special "affordable goal" and serving "underserved areas" (formerly inner-city areas). It established HUD (but not OFHEO) as the mission regulator. The mission goals essentially gave the GSEs a mandate to purchase lower-quality mortgages. These riskier mortgages received the same implicit government guarantee nevertheless.

While chapter 1 laid out the growth of Fannie and Freddie during the past 30 years, this chapter provides evidence of their increasing use of riskier mortgages from the mid-1990s until 2003, as a result of (or at least justified by) the 1992 act.

For good reason, many analysts point to the behavior of Fannie and Freddie in 2004–7 when it comes to ramping up the risk of their portfolio. But, as a matter of fact, the seeds for this behavior and the GSEs' eventual collapse started a decade earlier. Analysts, regulators, and politicians, however, did not realize that the GSEs were a ticking time bomb because aggregate U.S. housing prices increased every month from July 1995 to May 2006, thus obscuring the ever-increasing credit risk that Fannie and Freddie were taking on.

2.1 THE "MISSION" TO SUPPORT AFFORDABLE HOUSING

The new mission laid out in FHEFSSA was quite specific and encompassed three related goals for the GSEs. The overarching theme was for the GSEs to reach a target percentage of their mortgage purchases in terms of home ownership for lower- and middle-income households. The first goal was directed toward low-income housing, defined as household incomes that were below the area median. The second goal chose underserved areas as defined by census tracts with median household incomes that were less than 90% of the area median, or else in census tracts with a minority population of at least 30% and with a tract median income of less than 120% of the area median income. The final goal, named "special affordable housing," targeted census tracts with family incomes less than 60% of the area median (or else in tracts with incomes less than 80% of the area median and also located in specified low-income areas).[1] Table 2.1 provides the detailed goals for 1993 and after.

Until the late 1990s, Fannie and Freddie were mostly part of the general process of encouraging people who would buy anyway to buy more house on a larger lot. And they were doing most of their business in upper-income communities. As Jonathan Brown explains in Peter Wallison's book *Serving Two Masters, Yet Out of Control*, Fannie and Freddie were doing little business in

TABLE 2.1
GSE Affordable Housing Goals since 1993 (percentage of mortgage purchases)

	1993–1995	1996	1997–2000	2001–2004	2005	2006	2007	2008
Low- and moderate-income goal	30	40	42	50	52	53	55	56
Underserved areas goal	30	21	24	31	37	38	38	39
Special affordable goal	NA*	12	14	20	22	23	25	27

Source: Federal Housing Finance Agency.

*NA = not applicable: goals set in dollar amounts for each GSE rather than percentages.

the "inner city" where poor households tended to live and more business in the suburbs. These patterns led HUD in 2004 to step up the targets, which in turn, led Fannie and Freddie to undertake a greater proportion of high-risk mortgages. This increase followed on the heels of a large increase in targets in 2001.

It is an interesting counterfactual question to ask whether the GSEs' foray into risky lending would have occurred without these mission goals. In other words, in their desire to expand, would they still have moved along the increasingly risky mortgage credit curve? We believe that, given the GSEs' cheap source of financing and weak regulatory oversight, they would still have moved in this direction. Nevertheless, FHEFSSA made the point somewhat moot.

To reach the targets, FHEFSSA called for a study of the "implications of implementing underwriting standards that (A) establish a down payment requirement for mortgagors of 5 percent or less, (B) allow the use of cash on hand as a source for down payments, and (C) approve borrowers who have a credit history of delinquencies if the borrower can demonstrate a satisfactory credit history for at least the 12-month period ending on the date of the application for the mortgage."[2] A study commissioned by HUD in 2002 found that, over the previous decade, Fannie Mae and Freddie Mac had in fact adopted more flexible underwriting guidelines in terms of (A)–(C).[3] While the HUD report was describing these changes in Fannie's and Freddie's underwriting as a success, the report provides confirmation of the impact of FHEFSSA. Examples of such underwriting practices include Fannie Mae's introduction of its Flex 97 product, which required a borrower with a strong credit history to make only a 3% down payment.

2.2 RISKY BUSINESS

As the mortgage-backed securities (MBS) market took off in the 1980s, Fannie and Freddie dominated the growth in this market as a result of their government support. The credit-risk profile of Fannie's and Freddie's mortgages in those days, however, was reasonably safe: low- to medium-sized loans, loan-to-value ratios less than 80%, high standards for a borrower's creditworthiness, and income documentation of the borrower's ability to make interest payments on the loans. This does not mean that Fannie and Freddie were not without risk. But many analysts and economists at the time considered the greater source of risk to be the interest rate risk of Fannie's and Freddie's mortgage portfolio, not the credit risk of their portfolio plus their outstanding MBS.

But something dramatically changed with FHEFSSA. While the 1992 act required Fannie and Freddie to hold only conforming mortgages, there was considerable wiggle room. A conforming mortgage had to be less than a certain dollar amount (the "conforming loan limit"), have a loan-to-value ratio (LTV) less than 80% (or, with wiggle space, a higher LTV with private mortgage insurance), and meet unspecified "investment quality standards." Not surprisingly, these housing goals, combined with the ambiguity of what constitutes a conforming mortgage, translated into considerably riskier credit portfolios.

As an illustration of this, consider data on Fannie Mae's year-by-year mortgage purchases over the next decade from 1992 onward. While complete data are not available, figure 2.1, using the annual reports of Fannie and Freddie and recently released data by the FHFA, graphs the share of risky mortgage loans each year, as defined by either LTV > 90% or 80% < LTV < 90%.[4] While it was commonly known that the FHA and VA made risky loans, it is less known that Fannie (and Freddie) already had a growing presence in the high LTV mortgage market during the 1990s. Fannie's role generally increased over the next several years in both dollar amounts and market share. For example, from just 6% ($11.6 billion) of loans having LTVs > 90% in 1992, by 1995, the number of loans with LTVs > 90% had doubled to $20.9 billion and 19% of Fannie Mae's purchases. Though the percentage of loans with LTVs > 90% dropped to 13% by 2001, the dollar amounts increased substantially to $68.3 billion.

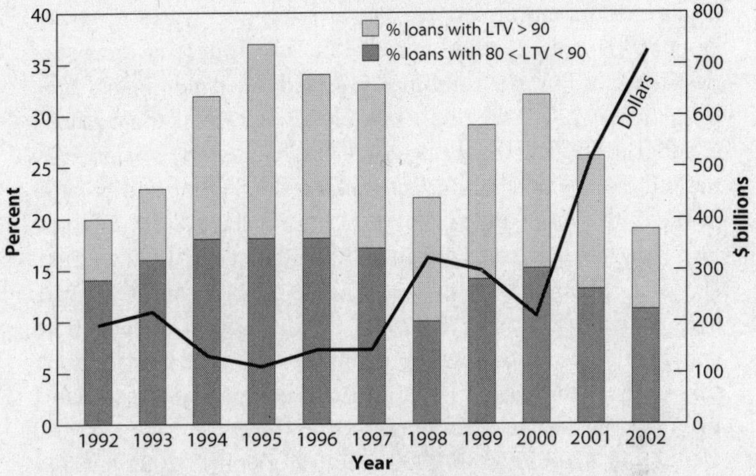

Figure 2.1: Fannie Mae Mortgage Purchases with High LTVs (1992–2002). *Source:* Annual reports of Fannie Mae, *Inside Mortgage Finance*

While Freddie Mac's annual reports provide only a snapshot of its mortgage holdings by year, the data tell a similar story. For example, in 1992 its mortgage book held just 3% of its loans with original LTVs > 90% (and 13% with 80% < LTV < 90%). The next year, this number increased to 4% and 15%, respectively, and by 1994 to 9% and 18%. By the late 1990s, the number had steadied to around 10% of loans with LTVs > 90% and 15% with 80% < LTV < 90%.

As corroborating evidence, consider data on Fannie's and Freddie's mortgage holdings and insurance guarantees starting from the mid-1990s that have been put together by Ed Pinto, the former chief credit officer of Fannie Mae (1987–89).[5] He provides data and analysis of two series: loans based on LTV, and loans based on FICO scores.[6] His data on LTV-based loans are generally consistent with the data in figure 2.1. The second series, that of "subprime" mortgage loans, makes an even stronger case for the earlier involvement by the GSEs in risky lending. While the mere mention of subprime now brings up an immediate negative connotation, subprime loans are generally considered to be ones that were granted to individuals with poor credit histories. The Pinto dataset combines so-called self-denominated subprime loans (i.e., those originated by subprime lenders or placed in subprime MBS) and loans with FICO credit scores below 660, the minimum threshold for standards set by Fannie and Freddie in the mid-1990s.[7] Pinto shows that the dollar volume of these loans hovered between $200 and $300 billion from 1997 to 2000, and, like the high LTV market, Fannie, Freddie, and the FHA held a significant share (ranging from 50–60%), with Fannie and Freddie contributing approximately one-half. For the next three years, Fannie's and Freddie's risky lending and private-label mortgage-backed security purchases (in terms of FICO < 660) went from $76 billion in 2000 to $175 billion in 2001 to $244 billion in 2002, with a 50% market share.

2.3 CROSSING THE RUBICON

The Rubicon River marks the boundary between the province of Gaul and Italy. It was Roman law that no general could cross this boundary southward toward Rome with his army, lest the general be mistaken for instigating a coup d'état. On January 10, 49 B.C., Julius Caesar did just that, stating the infamous words "alea jacta est" (the die is cast). And history was forever changed.

The entry of Fannie and Freddie into high-risk mortgages had a similar effect. The primary concern of their critics had been that of interest rate risk. Both GSEs held hundreds of billions of dollars of long-term fixed-rate mortgages in their portfolios. They funded these mortgages to a large extent with debt that had shorter maturities. Both GSEs claimed that they had engaged in derivative (interest rate swaps and options) transactions so as to eliminate any significant interest rate risk from their overall asset-liability positions. But the specifics of the hedging were murky, and critics were doubtful.

At the same time, however, the credit risks on the mortgages that the GSEs bought (and either held or securitized) were not considered a problem. The GSEs had a reputation for high underwriting standards, and their loss experiences supported this view. Except for a few years in the early 1970s for Freddie Mac, the credit loss experience of the GSEs had always been below the "guarantee fees" that they were charging on the MBS that they issued.

This observation ignored two important facts:

1. Before the mid-1990s, the GSEs guaranteed only safe conforming mortgages with generally low LTVs, good income coverage, and borrowers with high credit scores. So, even with small-to-medium downturns in the economy, mortgage defaults were not that likely.
2. After the mid-1990s, while the GSEs' mortgage underwriting standards deteriorated and their mortgages became much riskier, there was no housing downturn, and there was only one mild recession in 2001. In fact, from July 1995 to May 2006, the bellwether housing index of Case and Shiller increased by 196%, with no months experiencing a decline. Many analysts and politicians did not think that credit risk was an issue by mistakenly not taking into account the fact that homeowners do not default (i.e., if necessary, they sell) if their underlying house collateral has appreciated in value.

Point 2 is important. Common wisdom is that Fannie Mae and Freddie Mac blew up because of their risky behavior with respect to 2006 and 2007 mortgage vintages, which consisted in a significant measure of high-risk mortgages. The 2009 credit reports of Fannie show, for instance, that in 2007, it had as much as 25% of its loans with LTV above 80% and 18% with FICO score below 660, and in 2006 it had as much as 22.5% in subprime and similarly high-risk mortgages and 15.2% in interest-only loans. It is certainly true that the majority of GSE losses derived from these vintages. But the losses were confined to 2006 and 2007 vintages not because of prudent lending in prior years but instead because weaker loans in earlier years were masked by the continued rise in housing prices through mid-2006. Mortgages issued in 2003 and 2004 may have been just as shoddy, but homeowners had built substantial equity in their homes by 2006 because of the large house price increases, which protected them (and Fannie and Freddie) against the subsequent price decreases.

In other words, the GSEs had crossed their own Rubicon in the mid-1990s after the passage of FHEFSSA. The moment that the GSEs lowered their underwriting standards, there was no turning back, and as soon as housing prices started falling, their fate was sealed.

A final observation is that the GSE Affordable Housing Goals were all stipulated as a percentage of their mortgage purchase share. There were no growth targets. In fact, as figure 1.1 shows, their mortgage portfolios remained steady in size during 2003–7. It was the MBS guarantee business that truly took off. The government push for affordable housing does not explain why the GSEs chose to grow the MBS guarantee business so dramatically. While their first master, HUD, might have been unhappy with a lack of growth, their second master, the GSEs' shareholders, would have been even unhappier because investment banks had started generating substantial returns in lines of business that the GSEs were active in. This is the issue that we turn to next.

3

RACE TO THE BOTTOM

> "You're becoming irrelevant," Mr. Mozilo, CEO of Countrywide told Mr. Mudd, CEO of Fannie Mae, "You need us more than we need you, and if you don't take these loans, you'll find you can lose much more."
>
> —*Charles Duhigg,* New York Times, *October 5, 2008*

In their important 1932 book on the American corporation, *The Modern Corporation and Private Property*, Adolf Berle and Gardiner Means introduce the concept "race to the bottom": the idea that competition can lead to a reduction of standards. While Berle and Means were referring to regulatory standards and competition among the (then) 48 states, it is not difficult to see how the same arguments could be applied to government-sponsored enterprises and likewise financial institutions.

Figure 3.1 graphs the tremendous growth in the mortgage market (solid line, plotted against the right axis), and the fraction of residential mortgage originations each year that were securitized by the GSEs or private-label firms, as well as the amount not securitized (dashed lines plotted against the left axis). As can be seen from figure 3.1, the mortgage market increased dramatically in size, especially in the latter period with the emergence of

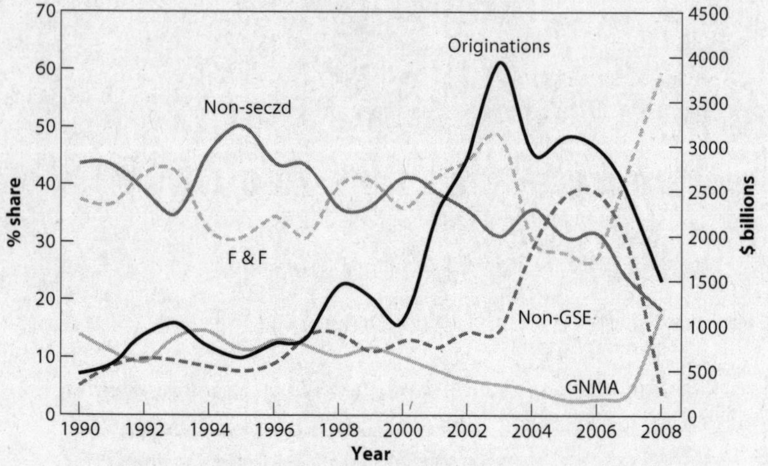

Figure 3.1. Growth in Mortgage Market, Securitization, and Percent Share of Market. *Source: Inside Mortgage Finance*

the riskier mortgage lending. It also shows that mortgage securitization generally increased every year from 1995 onward, albeit for different reasons. In the period up to 2003, the GSEs dominated the market, but, then post 2003, non-GSE MBS more than tripled from 12% to 38% of the origination market. By 2006 and 2007, figure 3.1 illustrates well the competitive struggle as the GSEs recovered some of their market share (and currently dominate the market).

The housing boom that began in the late 1990s and the concomitant rise of "private-label mortgage-backed securities" (PLS) shown in figure 3.1 posed a challenge to the GSEs. This is because the PLS involved nonconforming mortgages (securitized, for instance, by investment banks) that were of lower quality than the mortgages that met the GSEs' usual underwriting standards or were for amounts that exceeded the GSE conforming loan limit. Borrowers who might otherwise have qualified for a conforming loan were being encouraged by lenders to borrow greater amounts (pushing them into "jumbo" territory) and/or to structure their loans in ways that would not meet the GSEs' underwriting standards (pushing them into the nonconforming territory). The latter was done, for example, by the borrower's making less than the requisite 20% down payment but not arranging for private mortgage insurance, or by getting a second mortgage loan to cover some or even all of the down payment, or by getting an initial low "teaser" interest rate but with a scheduled upward adjustment after two or three years.

Chapter 2 described the increasingly risky mortgage profile of Fannie and Freddie from the mid-1990s through 2003. After 2003, faced with more competition and a declining market share (and, after accounting scandals in 2003 and 2004, limited in their ability to expand their portfolios and leverage), the GSEs continued to lower their underwriting standards to try to keep pace with the PLS market. While we argued in chapter 2 that even without this "race to the bottom," the GSEs would most likely have failed, it is certainly true that it would not have happened in such spectacular fashion and on such a scale. This chapter lays out the case.

3.1 GOLD RUSH

The housing boom that ended in the worst financial crisis since the Great Depression was a nationwide phenomenon. It started as far back as the mid-1990s. While local housing downturns (in Boston, New York, and Los Angeles, among other cities) led the national house price index to decline modestly between 1990 and 1995, since then house prices recorded an unprecedented run-up. The Case-Shiller 10-city index almost tripled from 77 in June 1996 to a high of 226 in June 2006—an increase of 11.3% per year. House price increases in some markets in Florida, Arizona, Nevada, and California were higher still.

This period was also one of fast-rising income and financial wealth inequality. Incomes of the middle class hardly increased, after controlling for the increase in the cost of living. Because house prices rose much faster than did median income, houses became much less affordable during the boom. Relative to the cost of renting, national house prices also increased substantially: by 31% to 43% from 2000 to the middle of 2006, depending on the data source. Households resorted to taking on more debt to afford their homes, and they also borrowed more against the rising value of their homes. Household mortgage debt increased from 54% of gross domestic product (GDP) at the end of 1996 to 89% of GDP at the end of 2006. This 10-year increase in household leverage was bigger than the entire increase from 1951 to 1996.

What caused this unprecedented boom in house prices? We believe various factors conspired, with no one single cause. The run-up took place in a favorable macroeconomic environment with low (real) interest rates (especially before 2005), low volatility, high economic growth (3.1% per year real GDP growth in 1985–2007), and low unemployment (especially after 2003). GDP growth was fueled by massive residential investment: construction grew by 225% from 2002 until 2005, as 2 million new houses came online each year. Short-term interest rates were kept low by the Federal Reserve through monetary stimulus that was aimed to fight the jobless recovery after the 2001 recession. An additional force that kept (long-term) interest rates low was the massive purchase spree of U.S. Treasuries and Agencies by foreign investors—something that Ben Bernanke dubbed the "global savings glut." Low mortgage interest rates induced households to refinance their homes and to take out home equity lines of credit to tap into their home equity.

But arguably the more important factor was the "financial liberalization" in housing finance that was underway, making it easier to get a mortgage for first-time home buyers and making it easier and cheaper for existing homeowners to tap into the equity in their home. And there was the securitization process, which made it easier for banks to offload the mortgage loans that they issued by selling those loans to others. Any erosion of adequate pricing and controls for risk along the securitization conveyor belt meant that it would be easier for mortgage originators to lend more and "farther down the quality curve."

3.2 IT'S THE UNDERWRITING, STUPID

There is no doubt that one reason for the increase in house prices clearly lies in the wider availability of mortgage credit through lower down payment requirements and lower costs that were associated with extracting equity from one's home. Homeowners could borrow more, and more easily, against the value of the house, and they could consume more easily out of their home equity. They responded to these new opportunities and massively increased their debt. Total household debt increased from 73% of GDP in the first quarter of 1996 to 111% in the fourth quarter of 2006. From 2001 to 2006, new mortgage originations totaled $18 trillion, or $3 trillion per year. Figure 3.1 describes the growth in the nonprime mortgage market from the mid-1990s on. Table 3.1 provides detailed origination data for the various segments of the mortgage market from 2001 to 2006.[1]

The development of the nonprime (low credit quality) mortgage market, including the market for home equity lines of credit, was an important aspect of this unprecedented housing credit expansion. Subprime and Alt-A mortgages were virtually nonexistent before the late 1990s.[2] They opened a new market for lower-income households, households with blemished credit records, or households with incomplete income documentation, none of which qualified for the conforming mortgages bought by the GSEs. The subprime share in originations was 8.5% in 2001–3 but then rose rapidly to 20% in 2005–6. The combination of subprime, Alt-A, and home equity lines of credit resulted in the extension of more than $1 trillion of nonprime mortgage debt in each of 2004, 2005, and 2006. The nonprime share increased from 14% to 48% of originations. Conforming mortgage originations—the raw material of the GSE-backed loan pools—fell from 58% to 33% of originations over this period.

TABLE 3.1
U.S. Mortgage Market Originations, 2001–2006 ($ in billions)

	Conforming	Jumbo	FHA/VA	Subprime	Alt-A	HELOCs	Total	ARM	Refinance	Nonprime
2001	1,280	450	175	120	60	130	2,215	16%	59%	14%
2002	1,711	576	176	185	67	170	2,885	24%	63%	15%
2003	2,460	650	220	310	85	220	3,945	26%	72%	16%
2004	1,210	510	130	530	185	355	2,920	50%	52%	37%
2005	1,090	570	90	625	380	365	3,120	48%	50%	44%
2006	990	480	80	600	400	430	2,980	45%	45%	48%

Source: Inside Mortgage Finance.

Many of these subprime and Alt-A loans were adjustable-rate mortgages (ARMs) with low initial teaser rates that were due to reset in 2007–9. The overall ARM share increased from 16% to 45%. These resets were typically associated with large increases in monthly payments and would later trigger a wave of foreclosures.

The expansion of mortgage credit to lower-income households was accompanied by a gradual erosion of lending standards. Combined loan-to-value ratios (CLTVs) increased for both prime and nonprime loans, and for both ARMs and fixed-rate mortgages (FRMs). There was a dramatic growth in the *fraction of loans whose CLTV exceeded 80%* in all three major loan categories. For prime ARMs, the fraction increased from 4.1% in 2002 to 26.2% in 2006, while for Alt-A ARMs, it increased from 20.8% to 55.5%, and for subprime ARMs from 46.8% to 64.0%. Importantly, these numbers underestimate the true problem because many houses were appraised too richly.

There also was dramatic growth in the fraction of loans that were *interest only* in all three major loan categories. For prime ARMs the fraction increased from 46% in 2002 to 91% in 2006, for Alt-A ARMs it increased from 26% to 87%, and for subprime ARMs the fraction increased from 1% to 20%. Moreover, the fraction of loans with full documentation (e.g., income verification) declined by more than 10 percentage points in all ARM categories. These so-called NINJA (no income, no job, and no assets) or "liar" loans turned out to be just that: loans with overstated income or assets showed much larger loan delinquencies during the crisis.

Finally, there was substantial growth in the average mortgage-payment-to-income ratio of households that held ARMs. In 2006 these averages were 37% for prime, 38% for Alt-A, and 42% for subprime ARM borrowers. A mortgage-payment-to-income ratio of 35% is considered high. The statistics for FRM holders are similar, except that they had a smaller fraction of incomplete documentation loans.

Loan quality continued to decline in 2007. According to a survey by the National Association of Realtors, the median down payment on home purchases was 9% in 2007, down from 20% in 1989; 29% of buyers put no money down; and many borrowed more than the price of the home to cover closing costs.

3.3 KING KONG VERSUS GODZILLA

While Freddie Mac had been securitizing mortgages since 1971 (and Fannie Mae since 1981), as explained in chapter 1, private-label securitization did not start in earnest until the mid-1990s. As seen in figure 3.1, in 1996, nonagency mortgage-backed securities (MBS) represented only 12% of all MBS originations. Their share grew dramatically from 17% in 2003 to 50% by 2006. In 2007, it fell back to 40%. Subprime mortgages were being securitized at a much higher rate than the average. In 2001, 50% of all subprime mortgages were securitized, whereas in 2006 this fraction had grown to 80%.

Was the growth in private-label MBS the culmination of the dream of the deregulation advocates of the 1980s coming to fruition, albeit two decades later? Or was it the emergence of new government-sponsored enterprises in the form of too-big-to-fail financial institutions? We argue the latter, and, with this emergence, came a battle between the GSEs and the too-big-to-fail large complex financial institutions (LCFIs), along with a race to the bottom in mortgage finance.

We argued in chapter 1 that no private firm could compete with Fannie and Freddie because of Fannie's and Freddie's access to government guaranteed capital. So how did the competitive race to the bottom play out till it all ended? One way that the private sector started competing was through moving down the credit curve of increasingly shaky mortgage loans—loans that were difficult for Fannie and Freddie to compete with, given their "conforming loan" underwriting standards. But this is not the whole story, as it still does not explain why anyone would purchase high-risk MBS in the first place.

The standard argument in the media is that securitization markets failed because originators and private-firm securitizers of mortgages did not have skin in the game, and naive investors—such as the proverbial Norwegian village—were left holding the bag. But the evidence does not bear this out. A Lehman Brothers study from 2008 showed that more than 50% of AAA-rated non-GSE MBS were held within the financial sector, which was highly concentrated in just a few LCFIs. For example, in June 2007, just before the start of the financial crisis, a dozen firms held almost two-thirds of all of the assets of the top 100 firms ($21 trillion) and constituted a "who's who" of the crisis that subsequently emerged: in order, Citigroup, Bank of America, JP Morgan Chase, Morgan Stanley, Merrill Lynch, AIG, Goldman Sachs, Fannie Mae, Freddie Mac, Wachovia, Lehman Brothers, and Wells Fargo. (Bear Stearns and Washington Mutual come in at No. 15 and 17, respectively.) All of these LCFIs were actively engaged in the mortgage market, and, of these 14 firms, one could convincingly argue that at least 9 of them either failed or were about to fail in the absence of government intervention.

Of course, the GSE firms and these LCFIs were not identical in form. The LCFIs had a more diversified product line, were afforded greater flexibility, and increasingly were perceived to have a too-big-to-fail government guarantee, whereas the GSEs had a public mission, received a more explicit government guarantee, and were subject to lighter capital requirements. But when one digs beneath the surface, the failure of the LCFIs and the GSEs is quite similar—a highly leveraged bet on the mortgage market by firms that were implicitly backed by the government with artificially low funding rates only to differing degrees.

Unlike Freddie and Fannie, however, these LCFIs had to resort to regulatory arbitrage tricks, in particular:

1. They funded portfolios of risky mortgage loans via off-balance-sheet vehicles (conduits and special investment vehicles [SIVs])

that received favorable capital treatment under the Basel capital standards for banks.

2. They made outright purchases of AAA-tranches of nonprime securities, which were treated as having low credit risk and zero liquidity and funding risk.
3. They enjoyed further capital relief on AAA-tranches if they bought "underpriced" protection on securitized products from monoline insurance companies and AIG (which were not subject to similar prudential standards).
4. In August 2004 investment banks successfully lobbied the SEC to amend the net capital rule of the Securities Exchange Act of 1934, which effectively allowed for leverage to increase in return for greater supervision.[3]

As is well documented now by the crisis, credit rating agencies provided inflated ratings to MBS and other asset-backed securities. These inflated ratings allowed increasingly risky credits to receive beneficial capital treatment. Specifically, because AAA-rated securities were given special status with respect to capital requirements, financial institutions such as Federal Deposit Insurance Corporation (FDIC)-insured depository institutions, too-big-to-fail institutions, and LCFIs, all with artificially low costs of funding because of explicit or implicit government guarantees—much like Fannie Mae and Freddie Mac—had a particular incentive to lever up on these AAA-rated securities.[4]

Tables 3.2 and 3.3 highlight this race to the bottom. Table 3.2 shows the total asset growth (relative to 2003) and equally weighted leverage (assets divided by shareholder's equity) for the five largest commercial banks (Citigroup, JPMorgan, Wells Fargo, Bank of America, and Wachovia), five largest investment banks (Goldman Sachs, Morgan Stanley, Merrill Lynch, Lehman Brothers, and Bear Stearns), and the two largest GSEs (Fannie Mae and Freddie Mac) in the United States during the period 2003 to 2007. Table 3.3 shows the return on assets (ROA)—an accounting measure of overall profitability of the firm, and return on equity

TABLE 3.2

Total Asset Growth and Equally Weighted Leverage of the Top Five U.S. Commercial Banks, Top Five U.S. Investment Banks, and GSEs

	Asset Growth Relative to 2003			Leverage		
Year	Commercial Banks	Investment Banks	Fannie-Freddie	Commercial Banks	Investment Banks	Fannie-Freddie
2003	1.0	1.0	1.0	13.4	23.0	28.2
2004	1.3	1.3	1.0	11.8	24.0	25.8
2005	1.4	1.5	0.9	11.9	24.5	25.3
2006	1.7	1.8	0.9	11.8	27.3	24.2
2007	1.9	2.1	0.9	12.6	30.9	23.8

Source: Fortune and authors' calculations. 2003 assets are normalized to 1.0 in all sectors. Leverage is defined as book assets to shareholder equity.

TABLE 3.3

Equally Weighted Return on Assets and Return on Equity of the Top Five U.S. Commercial Banks, Top Five U.S. Investment Banks, and GSEs (%)

	Return on Assets (ROA)			Return on Equity (ROE)		
Year	Commercial Banks	Investment Banks	Fannie-Freddie	Commercial Banks	Investment Banks	Fannie-Freddie
2003	1.3	0.7	0.7	17.5	14.7	20.3
2004	1.1	0.7	0.5	12.7	15.8	11.1
2005	1.3	0.7	0.6	15.7	16.8	12.2
2006	1.3	0.8	0.4	15.1	22.1	9.2
2007	0.8	0.2	-0.3	10.2	6.6	–8.2

Source: Fortune and authors' calculations.

(ROE)—an accounting measure of the performance of just the equity of the firm, again for these three sets of financial firms.

In a competitive race to the bottom involving financial risk taking, we would expect that firms expand their balance sheets (and off-balance-sheet positions if faced with on-balance-sheet constraints), do so increasingly with leverage, and finance assets that have an increasingly risky profile. Their economic performance as a whole—debt and equity combined—does not rise, and because of the undertaking of excessive risks, may even decline. However, the performance of their equity rises—both because of higher risk that pays off in good times and because of greater leverage. As the bets go bad, equity loses value first, resulting in sharp drops in its ROE.

These economic forces play out in tables 3.2 and 3.3, when viewed in combination with figure 3.1:

1. Investment banks and commercial banks grew their balance sheets by a factor of two between 2003 and 2007. When off-balance-sheet activities of some commercial banks (especially Citigroup) are taken into account, this growth is even higher. Interestingly, Fannie and Freddie did not grow much in terms of their on-balance-sheet assets over this period and in fact shrunk somewhat. They were constrained in their asset growth (and leverage) by their prudential regulator (OFHEO) after the accounting scandals of 2003–4. This, however, is misleading because their off-balance-sheet growth was not reined in. As figure 1.1 (and figure 3.1) show, their extension of MBS guarantees grew by a factor of two as well. All in all, the largest financial firms were willing to hold and guarantee mortgages and MBS at a pace hitherto unseen.
2. Investment banks started with a leverage of around 23:1, slightly lower than that of Fannie and Freddie but rocketed steadily toward a leverage exceeding 30 (Bear Stearns and Lehman Brothers being the most levered investment banks). In contrast, commercial bank leverage stood steady in the range of 10:1 to 15:1, which was consistent with a capital requirement of 8–10% for

being well capitalized. Citigroup, however, was levered close to 20:1 by 2007. Again, the leverage of commercial banks was significantly understated by their reported balance sheet figures, as they had engaged in a significant amount of off-balance-sheet vehicle guarantees.[5] And, while Fannie's and Freddie's book leverage in fact came down over this period because of pressures from the regulator, these leverage numbers did not capture the credit risk on their outstanding MBS, as well as the risk that mortgages were increasingly of worse quality over time. And all of these numbers also do not do justice to the fact that the risk in the financial sector was becoming all too concentrated on one asset class: housing.

3. What is telling, however, about this asset growth (and in the case of investment banks, leverage too) is that there was little improvement in the underlying economic profitability. During 2003–6 the ROA was steady for commercial banks, around 1.3%, and for investment banks, 0.7%-0.8%; and, in fact, for Fannie and Freddie it was declining steadily, from 0.7% to 0.4%. However, the ROE painted a different picture to the shareholders. Because commercial banks did not ramp up leverage that much, their ROE was steady in the range of 13% to 17%, that of investment banks kept rising with their leverage from 15% to 22%, and that of Fannie and Freddie in fact fell from 20% to 9%.

To summarize, banks (especially, investment banks) were growing aggressively during 2003–7 at a time when their underlying economic profitability was not improving. In parallel, Fannie and Freddie were growing aggressively (off balance sheet)—also in the face of declining profitability—yet could not compete with the private players in terms of generating comparable returns to shareholders. The substantial inflow of capital into the United States over this period—primarily in the form of holdings of Treasuries and agency debt, but which displaced domestic savings toward money-market funds and, in turn, as short-term borrowing for financial firms—facilitated the balance sheet expansion without much market scrutiny.[6] Thus, what had emerged in the financial sector was not a nimble, innovative set of mortgage finance firms but instead a highly distorted market with two types of institutions—LCFI King Kongs and GSE Godzillas—both implicitly backed by the government, growing at a feverish pace, with substantial leverage, fighting each other in risk taking all the way to the bottom while absorbing the massive inflows of capital into the United States.

When housing prices declined in 2007 and the tail risk that these institutions had betted against materialized, they all experienced substantial stress. Commercial banks by virtue of their steady profitability (ROA) and less aggressive leverage suffered the least, but even among them the most leveraged and risky—Citigroup—eventually had to be bailed out. Investment banks and Fannie-Freddie fell off the cliff, both because of lower profitability (ROA) and higher leverage. Leverage and risks—essential features that had helped them accelerate and pump up greater shareholder returns (ROE) in good times—accelerated their decline when the housing markets hit the wall.

3.4 ALL-IN

The preceding section describes a "race to the bottom" between large financial institutions with implicit government guarantees and the GSEs. Given their low cost of funding, the lack of any market discipline imposed by creditors, and the systemic risk being borne by society and not themselves, they took on increasingly risky mortgage loans with ever-greater leverage. And as a result, an ever-larger share of the mortgage market was low-quality mortgage loans, and an ever-larger share of those was being securitized instead of being held by the originators. Because the mortgage originator often did not hold on to the loan, the originator's incentives properly to evaluate the borrower and to monitor the loan after it was issued were reduced substantially.

The strong growth in private-label subprime mortgage originations and securitizations had important consequences for the GSEs. First, as shown in figure 3.1, their market share of originations fell dramatically between 2003 and 2006. Second, the loss in market share made it harder for them to meet their ever-increasing congressionally mandated quotas. To preserve the profit growth rates of the pre-2003 period and to simultaneously meet their quotas, the GSEs embarked on an all-in policy, which saw them dramatically ramp up the risks of their portfolio. This policy started as far back as 2000–2001 with the motivation that a stronger GSE presence in the subprime market would create lower priced mortgages for some subprime borrowers.

While there is little doubt that the housing goals played an important role in shifting Fannie Mae's and Freddie Mac's profile to riskier mortgage loans, it remains an interesting question whether Fannie Mae and Freddie Mac deliberately chose to increase the riskiness of the loans that they bought in 2004 onward or whether they were forced to do so by the U.S. Congress, which wanted to promote home ownership. While the public-private nature of the GSEs leads to a moral hazard problem even in normal times, the question is whether moral hazard was exacerbated by the astronomical growth of the subprime market segment.

As pointed out earlier in chapter 2, the GSEs saw consecutive increases in their low- and moderate-income, special affordability, and underserved areas goals in each of 1996, 1997, 2001, 2005, 2006, 2007, and 2008. However, the largest increases took place in 1996 and in 2001, outside of the rapid growth of the 2003 period and onward. Moreover, the target increases in 2005, 2006, and 2007 were more modest, yet that is when most of the increase in riskiness took place. Finally, Fannie and Freddie missed one or more of their mission targets on several occasions, without severe sanctions by the regulator, suggesting that adherence was largely voluntary.

Former FHFA director James Lockhart testified that both Fannie and Freddie "had serious deficiencies in systems, risk management, and internal controls." Furthermore, "there was no mission-related reason why the Enterprises needed portfolios that totaled $1.5 trillion." He chalked it up to "the Enterprises' drive for market share and short-term profitability." In fact, in testimony to the Financial Crisis Inquiry Commission on April 9, 2010, former Fannie Mae CEO Daniel Mudd admitted as much:

> In 2003, Fannie Mae's estimated market share of new single-family mortgage-related securities was 45%. By 2006, it had fallen to 23.7%. It became clear that the movement towards nontraditional products was not a fad, but a growing and permanent change in the mortgage marketplace, which the GSEs (as companies specialized in and limited to, the mortgage market) could not ignore.

Similar language can be found in Fannie Mae's own strategic plan document, "Fannie Mae Strategic Plan, 2007–2011, Deepen Segments—Develop Breadth," in which the company outlined its 2007 onwards strategy:

> Our business model—investing in and guaranteeing home mortgages—is a good one, so good that others want to 'take us out.' . . . Under our new strategy, we will take and manage more credit risk, moving deeper into the credit pool to serve a large and growing part of the mortgage market.

The data tell the story. As described in chapter 2, from 1992 to 2002, Fannie Mae and Freddie Mac were clearly major participants in high-risk mortgage lending. Nevertheless, the period 2003–7 represented a significant shift. Table 3.4 presents data for "risky" mortgage loans for both Fannie Mae/Freddie Mac and private-label securitization for this period. For comparison purposes, we restrict ourselves to the size of mortgages at or below the conforming-limit level. For example, from 2001 to 2003, for mortgage loans with LTVs greater than 80% and/or FICO scores less than 660, Fannie Mae and Freddie Mac represented respectively 86%, 80%, and 74% of this high-risk activity. From 2004–5, this changed as both the dollar volume and share of high-risk lending of conforming-size loans moved toward the private sector, with $168 billion (and a 26% share) in 2003 to $283 billion (and a 52% share) in 2004 and $330 billion (and 58% share) in 2005.

Consistent with the race to the bottom, Fannie and Freddie responded by increasing their high-risk mortgage participation by recovering a majority share of 51% in 2006 and an almost complete share of the market in 2007 at 87%. Equally important, as a percentage of their own business, table 3.4 shows that Fannie's and Freddie's risky mortgage share increased from 25% in 2003 to 36% in 2007. Even more telling, if the preceding analysis is restricted to the very highest-risk mortgage loans, that is, those with LTVs > 90% *and* FICO < 620, table 3.4 shows an almost identical "race-to-the-bottom" pattern in Fannie's and Freddie's share during the 2003–7 period, culminating in a doubling of these particularly risky mortgages from $10.4 billion in 2006 to $20.3 billion in 2007.[7]

On top of this high-risk lending activity, table 3.4 also provides evidence that Fannie and Freddie grew their mortgage portfolio as the race to the bottom unfolded. For example, compared to $103 billion of risky private-label MBS purchased in 2003, over the next three years, Fannie and Freddie averaged $204 billion per year even though their overall MBS purchases essentially halved. In other words, their percentage share in risky MBS for their own portfolio quadrupled over this period.

The SEC 10-K credit-risk filings of Fannie Mae are also revealing of the deterioration in mortgage loans that were purchased by the GSEs during the 2004–7 period, either for their own portfolios or to be sold off to others. For example, 17% of the 2006 and 25% of the 2007 mortgages that Fannie bought had a loan-to-value ratio in excess of 80%. The fraction of loans with CLTVs greater than 95% went from 5% in 2004 to 15% in 2007. The borrowers also had lower credit scores: 17.4% of 2006 loans and 18% of 2007 loans had FICO scores below 660. A relatively large share comprised ARMs (16.6% in 2006 and 9% in 2007)

TABLE 3.4
The Increasingly Risky GSE Lending Activity, 2003–2007 ($ in billions)

	GSE New Business			GSE Mortgage Portfolio Purchases		Private Market New Business (Nonagency)			GSE High Risk	GSE Share in High-Risk Activity
	High Risk (1) LTVs > 80% and/or FICO < 660	Very High Risk LTVs > 90% and FICO < 620	Total (2)	Private-Label Securities (PLS)	PLS/ Total	High Risk (3) LTVs > 80% and/or FICO < 660 Conforming Limit	Very high risk LTVs > 90% and FICO < 620 Conforming Limit	Total PLS	(1)/(2)	(1)/ [(1)+(3)]
2003	466	12.1	1,839	103.2	13%	168	8.9	527	25%	74%
2004	262	8.8	898	211.8	53%	283	14.1	804	29%	48%
2005	236	7.1	899	221.3	57%	330	13.9	1,139	26%	42%
2006	245	10.4	877	180	52%	240	12.4	1,108	28%	51%
2007	363	20.3	1,012	113.5	37%	54	2.4	665	36%	87%

Sources: Federal Housing Finance Agency, Office of Federal Housing Enterprise Oversight Annual Report, *Inside Mortgage Finance.*

Notes: GSE new business represents originated guaranteed MBS plus non-private-label MBS portfolio purchases; the private market new business represents all MBS financed through private-label securitization.

or interest-only loans (15.2% in both years). The Alt-A fraction of purchases was 21.8% in 2006 and 16.7% in 2007, up from 12% in 2004. Finally, non-full-documentation loans went from 18% in 2004 to 31% in 2007. If anything, Freddie Mac's credit-risk profile was worse than Fannie's. In 2004, 11% of the loans that Freddie bought had CLTVs above 100%, which increased to 37% by 2007. Interest-only loans grew from 2% to 20%, and low-FICO-score loans from 4% to 7%. As a final indication of its all-in approach to mortgage lending in 2007, note again that mortgage loans with both FICO < 620 and LTV > 90% reached $20.3 billion, essentially double that of any other year.

Clearly, the quality of GSE loans deteriorated substantially from 2003 to 2007. It seems that the GSEs were able to stretch the concept of a prime, conforming loan much beyond what its regulator had intended.

4

TOO BIG TO FAIL

> Once one agrees to share a canoe with a bear, it is hard to get him out without obtaining his agreement or getting wet.
>
> *—Congressional Budget Office, "Assessing the Public Costs and Benefits of Fannie Mae and Freddie Mac" (1996)*

On October 5, 1999, in a speech entitled "Toward a 21st Century Financial Regulatory System," then treasury secretary Lawrence Summers, and later director of the National Economic Council in the early Obama Administration, said: "Debates about systemic risk should also now include government-sponsored enterprises (GSEs), which are large and growing rapidly."

Several months later, on March 22, 2000, in remarks to the House Banking Committee, then treasury under-secretary Gary Gensler, who later became the chairman of the U.S. Commodity Futures Trading Commission, testified in support of HR 3703 Housing Finance Regulatory Improvement Act—a bill to rein in Fannie Mae and Freddie Mac, the largest of the GSEs: "As the GSEs continue to grow and to play an increasingly central role in the capital markets, issues of potential systemic risk and market competition become more relevant."

Publicly expressing concerns about the growth in GSEs was somewhat of a mea culpa for the Clinton administration, as it had been a strong advocate for using the GSEs to push the public mission of affordable housing for low-income families. There was, however, reason to be worried. Over the eight years of the Clinton administration, Fannie Mae and Freddie Mac combined went from holding $153 billion in mortgages and guaranteeing the credit risk of another $714 billion to holding $993 billion and guaranteeing $1.28 trillion.[1] Yet no action was taken.

The task of dealing with the GSEs was left to the succeeding Bush administration, which too would adopt a split personality toward the GSE business model. On the one hand, the GSEs were a convenient way to further and support the "ownership" society, which was the mantra of the Bush administration. For example, on the presidential campaign trail, on October 2, 2004, in Cuyahoga Falls, Ohio, then President Bush stated:

> We're creating ... an ownership society in this country, where more Americans than ever will be able to open up their door where they live and say, welcome to my house, welcome to my piece of property.

On the other hand, increasing numbers of administration officials and appointees were sounding the alarm on the systemic risk of the GSEs:

> There is a general recognition that the supervisory system for housing-related government sponsored enterprises (GSEs) neither has the tools, nor the stature, to deal effectively with the current size, complexity, and importance of these enterprises. (September 10, 2003, Testimony of John W. Snow, secretary of the treasury, before the Committee on Financial Services, U.S. House of Representatives)

> The enormous size of the mortgage-backed securities market means that any problems at the GSEs matter for the financial system as a whole. (November 5, 2003, Gregory

Mankiw, chairman, Council of Economic Advisers, at the Conference of State Bank Supervisors State Banking Summit and Leadership Conference)

I have argued today that the size and the potentially rapid growth of GSE portfolios, combined with the lack of market discipline faced by GSEs, raise substantial systemic risk concerns. (March 6, 2007, Ben S. Bernanke, chairman of the Federal Reserve Board of Governors, at the Independent Community Bankers of America's Annual Convention)

Of course, we know how this story ends. Calls for better regulatory oversight and receivership regimes for the GSEs went unheeded. But it should have been clear from the outset that no credible resolution authority existed for the GSEs, because of the amount of systemic risk produced by them. The GSEs were in effect too big to fail.

4.1 SYSTEMIC RISK AND THE GSES

Systemic risk has been a term much used in the current financial crisis to describe "hazardous" financial institutions; but what exactly is it, and in what sense were the GSEs systemic?

Between the fall of 2008 and the winter of 2009, the world's economy and financial markets fell off a cliff. Stock markets in the United States, Asia, Europe, and Latin America lost between a third and half of their value; international trade declined by a whopping 12%; and the size of the global economy contracted for the first time in decades. When economists and Wall Street types toss around the term systemic risk, that's pretty much what they're talking about.

Systemic risk emerges when the financial sector at large does not have enough capital to cover either its debts or its bets. As a result, when those bets go sour and debts cannot be paid, many institutions fail or the credit markets freeze—and without credit, commerce plummets, and economies fall into recession. That is precisely what happened with some of our largest institutions in September and October of 2008: Lehman Brothers, AIG, Merrill Lynch, Washington Mutual, Wachovia, Citigroup, and, of course, the two largest GSEs, Fannie Mae and Freddie Mac.

What matters for understanding the systemic risk of any given financial institution is how much that firm contributes to an aggregate sector-wide failure. To determine how an individual firm contributes to systemic financial risk, we must be able to estimate the size and variability of its assets and liabilities, how the asset losses mirror those of the overall financial sector in a crisis, and how interconnected the institution is with the rest of the financial system. Except for this last factor, all can be calculated from publicly available data.

Indeed, with our colleagues at the Stern School of Business, we have created a systemic-risk ranking of the 100 largest financial firms historically through today (see, e.g., http://vlab.stern.nyu.edu/welcome/risk). As an illustration, on July 1, 2007, just before the financial crisis erupted, Fannie and Freddie were estimated together to hold 15.3% of the systemic risk in the system—an amount that was greater than any other financial institution. Even as the crisis spread and other firms became systemic, on March 1, 2008, just before the Bear Stearns collapse, these two GSEs combined captured 13%—again, an amount greater than any other financial firm. And in the week before being put into conservatorship, on August 31, 2008, Fannie and Freddie again show up as most systemic with a total contribution of 11.3%.

These numbers suggest the enormity of Fannie's and Freddie's systemic risk. But they obscure the underlying economics of their systemic-risk production. Generally, systemic risk can emerge in one of four ways:

1. *Counterparty risk:* If a financial institution is highly interconnected to many other financial institutions, then its failure can impose losses on others and have a ripple effect throughout the system.

2. *Systemically important financial market utilities and payment, clearing, and settlement activities:* If a firm operates or significantly owns a public utility function that participates in moving reserves (or any other financial claim that effectively serves the purpose of "money," such as money market deposits or repo contracts) around the economy, then its failure could cause a breakdown in economic activity.

3. *Runs:* Many financial institutions have fragile capital structures in that they hold assets with long-term duration or low liquidity, but their liabilities are highly short-term in nature, exposing these firms to individual runs on their liabilities that could, with enough uncertainty and given commonality of asset exposures, lead to large-scale runs on similar institutions.

4. *Fire sales:* With respect to fire sales, consider the spillover risk—what economists like to call a "pecuniary externality"—that arises as one institution's trouble leads to depressed asset prices and a hostile funding environment, pulling others down and thus leading to further price drops and funding problems, resulting in a "death spiral" in the financial sector.

We now consider each of these in turn as it relates to Fannie and Freddie. Consistent with what our systemic-risk rankings suggest, a valid economic argument can be made that no firm was systemically more important than the GSEs.

4.1.1 Interconnected to the Max

According to the American Cancer Society, this year, approximately 550,000 Americans are expected to die of cancer, which accounts for almost one of every four deaths. Contrary to common opinion, the initial onset of cancer—abnormal tissue growth that is called a tumor—is not what causes death. It is the breaking away of cells from the tumor that enter the bloodstream or lymphatic system and spread throughout the body, resulting in new tumors in vital areas. In other words, a small cancer in one part of the body, especially if untreated, can lead to widespread cancer and eventual death.

It is not much different in financial markets when one considers the failure of an interconnected financial institution. For example, consider the over-the-counter (OTC) derivatives market. The main reason for systemic risk in OTC markets is that individual institutions do not observe the totality of trades that are being done by their counterparties. The prime example in the current crisis is AIG, which built up $450 billion of one-sided credit default swap (CDS) exposure on the so-called AAA-tranches of securitized products. These positions were built up with no or little capital and collateral support. Because all of the trades were in the same direction, once the trades lost value, it meant that AIG's failure would be passed on throughout the financial system. For example, AIG's failure could cause an AIG counterparty to fail, one consequence of which could result in a counterparty to AIG's counterparty to fail even though that second firm has no direct relation to AIG, and so on. Thus, it is not AIG's failure that leads to the collapse of the financial system but the havoc caused by such a failure.

And to keep with the medical analogy, there was no greater cancerous growth than the GSEs. As we explained in chapter 2, they had a "mission" to expand and to serve the most vulnerable pocket of credit risk of the economy. And they were more interconnected than any other financial institution because of not only the size of their assets but also the depth of their activities, especially their mortgage guarantee business, their presence in OTC derivatives, and the banking sector's holdings of significant portions of the GSEs' debt obligations.

On March 3, 2009, after testimony to the U.S. Senate budget committee, and, in responding to a senator's questions on the bailout of AIG, Chairman Bernanke stated: "We have been doing what we can to break the company (AIG) up, to get it into a saleable position and try to defang it.... If there's a single episode in this entire 18 months that has made me more angry, I can't think of one (other than) AIG."

Chairman Bernanke is referring to the Financial Products Group at AIG that wrote the aforementioned $450 billion of CDS on AAA-rated products with little or no capital. His anger is understandable but perhaps should have been carried through to the GSEs as well. AIG's CDS positions were peanuts in comparison to the GSEs' writing $3.5 trillion worth of credit guarantees on much riskier assets—residential mortgages—and similarly with little capital (albeit in accordance with regulatory requirements) and all in one direction.

If Fannie and Freddie were allowed to fail, $3.5 trillion worth of guarantees held by the banking sector, pension and mutual funds, foreign governments, and other entities would now be in a state of flux. There was no bankruptcy procedure in place to say how these guarantees might be paid relative to the debt of Fannie and Freddie. All of this risk would be transferred immediately to counterparties who most likely had not allocated any risk capital for this purpose. And, by the way, this risk would be passed on during the greatest housing collapse in U.S. history. In addition to the high-profile collapse of Bear Stearns, by the time Fannie's and Freddie's insolvency was imminent, many of the nation's largest mortgage lenders had gone out of business or merged under distress, including IndyMac Bank, Countrywide Financial Corporation, and New Century Financial. Letting Fannie and Freddie fail would have been the equivalent of a financial "End of Days."

Though sufficient to top the systemic-risk charts, the mortgage guarantee business was not the only interconnection of the GSEs to the financial system. Fannie and Freddie presented considerable counterparty risk to the system through its large OTC derivatives book, similar in spirit to Long Term Capital

Management (LTCM) in the summer of 1998 and to the investment banks during this current crisis. While often criticized for not adequately hedging the interest rate exposure of their portfolios, Fannie and Freddie were nevertheless major participants in the interest rate swaps market. In 2007 Fannie and Freddie had a notional amount of swaps and OTC derivatives outstanding of $1.38 trillion and $523 billion, respectively.

The failure of Fannie and Freddie would have led to a winding down of large quantities of swaps with the usual systemic consequences. The mere quantity of transactions would have led to fire sales and invariably to liquidity funding problems for some of Fannie's and Freddie's OTC counterparties. Moreover, counterparties of Fannie and Freddie in a derivative contract might need to reintermediate the contract right away, as it might be serving as a hedge of some underlying commercial risks. Therefore, because of counterparties' liquidating the existing derivatives all at once and replacing their derivative positions at the same time, the markets would almost surely be destabilized as a result of the pure number of trades, required payment and settlement activity, and induced uncertainty and the fact that this was taking place during a crisis.

Finally, Fannie and Freddie were interconnected to the financial system because so many financial firms held significant portions of their debt obligations and guaranteed securities. Figure 4.1 plots the holders of Agencies and GSE-backed securities between 2003 and 2010. To get an idea of the magnitude, combining all of GSE debt and GSE-backed securities (and including the FHLB System and other GSEs), there was $8.1 trillion outstanding at the end of 2009, making this one of the largest fixed-income markets in the world. For comparison, the federal government owed $7.8 trillion, and all nonfinancial companies combined owed $7.1 trillion at the time. As is clear from the figure, the holdings of Fannie and Freddie debt and securities by the government (federal, but also state and local) and the Federal Reserve (starting in 2009) have been on the rise.

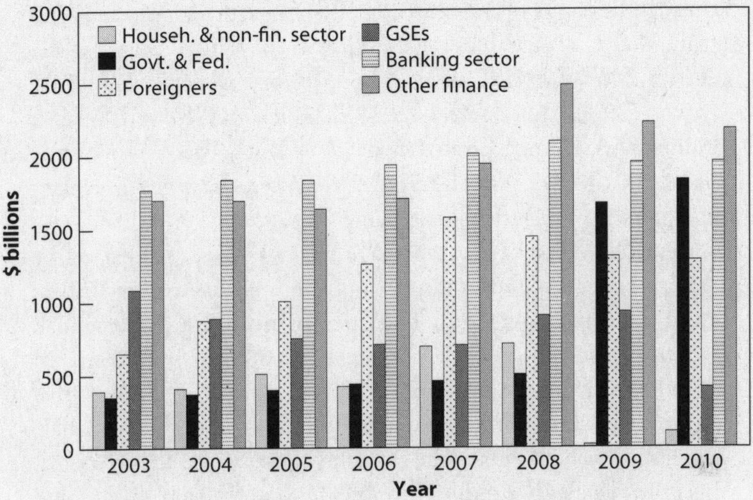

Figure 4.1: Holdings of Agency and GSE-backed Securities, in billions of U.S. dollars. Source: Federal Reserve, Flow of Funds, various Level Tables; 2010 numbers are for the first quarter. Government includes federal, state, and local. The banking sector includes commercial banks, savings institutions, credit unions, brokers and dealers, ABS issuers, and REITs. Other finance includes government and private retirement funds, money market and other mutual funds, as well as property, casualty insurance, and life insurance companies.

The financial sector holds more than half of these assets. Banks hold $1.6 trillion, broker-dealers $128 billion, and asset-backed security (ABS) issuers $113 billion. Focusing on just the debt obligations, according to the FDIC, insured banks and thrifts held almost 17% of Fannie's and Freddie's outstanding debt. Other financial companies holding GSE debt and securities are money market and other mutual funds, which hold $1.1 trillion; government and private retirement funds, which hold $559 billion; and insurance companies, which hold $480 billion. Given the size of these holdings, a default, or even a 10% loss in the value of these securities, could devastate the U.S. financial sector.

Commercial and investment banks were heavily exposed to mortgages through direct holdings of whole loans, but also through holdings of tranches of MBS. In particular, of the $10.7 trillion of mortgage debt outstanding in the United States at the end of 2007, the GSEs held $1.5 trillion and banks held $4.2 trillion (39%).[2] The banks held $852 billion in GSE MBS, $380 billion in AAA-rated tranches of non-GSE MBS, and $90 billion in below-AAA-rated tranches that were packaged in collateralized debt obligations (subprime CDOs).

In effect, a lot of the mortgage risk was never passed on by the banking sector to other areas of the financial system (insurance, asset managers, and foreigners). Instead, either the risk remained directly on the books of the banks, with AAA-rated tranches attracting a favorable capital treatment of 20% relative to similar-risk corporate loans, or the risk was held in off-balance-sheet vehicles that were set up by these banks. These "special purpose vehicles" ("conduits" and SIVs) were typically given some form of liquidity or credit guarantees by the bank that set them up—guarantees that were triggered during the crisis. Regulatory arbitrage made it profitable for banks to set up these off-balance-sheet structures and to earn the small excess return on AAA-rated MBS tranches compared to Treasuries.[3]

In addition, there is the special treatment of GSE debt as eligible collateral in the Federal Reserve's open-market operations and the statutory leniency that allowed banks and thrifts to hold unlimited quantities of the GSEs' debt. This meant that the banking sector had a preference for holding GSE debt as opposed to other assets because it allowed for much greater leverage and had "convenience yield" as liquid assets. Finally, all investors that held the GSE debt had assumed that the U.S. government would most likely—even if not surely—make good on these implicit promises, as suggested by the name "(government) agency" debt.

Of course, ironically, if the GSEs were not bailed out, and the debt losses were passed on to the banking sector, the losses would be all the more painful because little or no capital was held against the debt in the first place. In fact, the banking sector would be on the hook for more than $300 billion, albeit backed by the GSEs' mortgage portfolios. Given the impact of Lehman's failure on hedge funds and money market funds in particular, it is reasonable to assume that debt losses of the magnitude of the GSEs would have had far greater consequences and potentially triggered a run on the worst-hit firms, followed by a full-scale panic.

4.1.2 The Economy's Plumbing

About 250 feet below ground in New York City stand two large tunnels—one completed in 1917, the other in 1936. These tunnels carry more than 1¼ billion gallons of water a day from mountain reservoirs that are located well north of the city. The problem is that they are leaking more than 30 million gallons of water a day and are in desperate need of repair. Of course, the obvious solution would be to fix the leaks—in other words, to close the tunnel valves, enter the tunnels, and repair the damage. The problem is that if the valves are closed, engineers do not know for certain that they will be able to reopen them. And this would be catastrophic to New York: a loss of half of its water supply. It is no exaggeration to state that these two decaying tunnels provide infrastructure without which the city could not function. It should be no surprise then that, in lieu of another solution, New York City is working feverishly 600 feet below ground on Tunnel no. 3, a $6 billion project that is slated to be completed by 2020, which will carry water and allow work on the other tunnels. It is simply a race against time.

Similar to the giant tunnels under New York City, the financial sector also has become reliant on several institutions for its core "plumbing." As one illustration, while many analysts focus on the systemic risk that is produced by the large dealer banks with their massive over-the-counter derivatives books and risky trading operations, regulators at the Federal Reserve Bank of New York (NY Fed) fret and worry about the Bank of New York Mellon (BNY). BNY—the oldest bank in the United States, having been founded in 1784 by Alexander Hamilton no less—is certainly a large financial institution, and especially so in terms of custodial services and asset management. But this is not what worries the NY Fed. BNY is one of the two *triparty* clearing banks—the other being JP Morgan Chase—for the repo market.

As background, a repo is a secured loan in which one party borrows cash from another and pledges securities—U.S. Treasuries, Agencies, MBS, and other asset-backed securities—as collateral. However, repos backed by Treasuries, Agencies, and MBS are technically "sale and repurchase" transactions, in that the lenders can simply seize the underlying collateral in case of the borrower's default and remain exempt from any bankruptcy proceeding. Typical borrowers in repo markets are large financial institutions ("dealers") and typical lenders are money market funds and securities lenders ("cash investors"). They do not, however, execute their transactions directly with each other. Instead, BNY and JP Morgan Chase act as third parties in these transactions, providing intermediation services to the dealers and the cash investors. BNY and JP Morgan Chase, however, often provide a settlement of repo contracts to dealers *before* the settlement is complete with cash investors. In the process of providing such early settlement, they become exposed to dealers themselves on an intraday basis.[4]

At its peak, more than $2.8 trillion worth of securities were funded on an overnight basis through triparty repo transactions. But as the financial crisis took hold, because the clearing banks had a huge amount of exposure on an intraday basis, regulators worried that a failure of a major dealer could cause the clearing bank to falter, which in turn would cause the financial system to stop functioning. Like the New York City Department of Environmental Protection, the Federal Reserve cannot simply shut down the triparty repo market because the financial system relies on this market; instead, the Fed has been frantically trying to develop a new repo infrastructure before the next financial crisis causes it to fail.[5]

A similar argument can be made for the GSEs.

The mortgage finance market—the largest debt market in the United States serving a key economic function (i.e., housing)—had become almost completely dependent on the GSEs for financing mortgages. For example, in 2007, of the $2.43 trillion in new residential single-family mortgage loans, the GSEs purchased $1.13 trillion worth of mortgages, the majority of which were then guaranteed by the GSEs and issued as MBS to the capital market. And like our New York City water tunnel analogy, when the GSEs effectively failed in 2008, pulling the plug on the GSEs would have created a 50% sucking sound from the mortgage finance market. In fact, ironically, the GSEs have headed in the opposite direction. According to *Inside Mortgage Finance*, in the first half of 2010, Fannie Mae and Freddie Mac accounted for a whopping 64% of all single-family mortgage securities.

It is fairly clear that allowing the GSEs to fail would have disrupted the firms' ongoing MBS issue/guarantee business, with major consequences for the U.S. mortgage markets. In the context of the evolving subprime mortgage crisis, with virtually no ongoing private mortgage investment activity, the result would likely have been a systemic failure of the U.S. mortgage system with obvious dire consequences for the real economy.

But by no means is this evidence in favor of the GSE model. To the extent that mortgage originators can sell their loans to the GSEs, the originators have less incentive to monitor the loans. *Inside Mortgage Finance* reports that the three largest sellers to the GSEs during the 2002–6 period were Countrywide, Wells Fargo, and Washington Mutual—two of which received some notoriety during the crisis for poor loan quality.

Why did this problem exist? Originators make their fees either way; so as long as the GSEs purchase them, the originators don't care about quality. And why do investors purchase MBS issued by the GSEs? Because the GSEs guarantee the credit risk, investors don't face this risk, so they don't care about the poor loan quality either. But then why do the GSEs still buy these loans? Even though to a private-sector financial firm these loans are poor quality, the loans may still be worthwhile investments for the GSEs because they have access to cheap debt financing as a result of the implicit government guarantee. And, ironically, the more of these types of loans that they purchase, the more likely that the implicit guarantee becomes even stronger.

A poor loan here or there, a distortion once in a while, is not disastrous; but the implicit guarantee of the U.S. government allowed the GSEs to grow unencumbered for decades. The light regulatory capital requirements—2.50% for portfolio holdings and 0.45% for default guarantees—may have seemed reasonable when set back in 1992 (although they were lower than the comparable capital requirements for banks and thrifts, as was explained in chapter 1), but the mortgage-backed assets of the GSEs of 2007 had a far riskier credit profile than those of 15 years earlier.

In 1996 a Congressional Budget Office (CBO) study entitled "Assessing the Public Costs and Benefits of Fannie Mae and Freddie Mac" made the case for full privatization of the GSEs but recognized the problem of doing so when the economy had become so reliant on them. And this was back in 1996, not 2007. The report provides the analogy of the bear in the canoe with which we started this chapter.[6] Because the GSEs are currently under the conservatorship of the government, it would be crazy not to kill off the "bear" and move forward with a model that did not again create a too-big-to-fail—and, more likely, a too-big-to-reform—monster.

4.1.3 Running for the Exit

A senior executive at the now defunct Salomon Brothers used to say that when trading, never panic; but if you do panic, panic first.

A few months after the financial crisis had started, on September 14, 2007, a curious thing began to happen at the 76 branches of the U.K.-based firm Northern Rock. Right out of a scene from the Jimmy Stewart movie "It's a Wonderful Life," lines began to develop outside the bank branches as people began to withdraw their life savings. It was a classic run on the bank.

The triggering event was ironically the revelation that the Bank of England was going to provide financial support to Northern Rock. To regulators at the time, this financial support was intended to calm markets, and their view was that Northern Rock customers were panicking. But the truth is that, with any uncertainty about bank solvency or timely administration of the government support, it is rational for customers to "panic" first, withdraw their funds, and place them elsewhere. Of course, everyone thinks that way, and a run starts. In an article describing the run on Northern Rock in *The Sunday Times*, this point is perhaps best illustrated by one particular savings customer lining up outside a branch: "I don't want to be the mug left without my savings."[7]

As Fannie and Freddie were running aground in early September 2008, and the issue was whether or not to confirm what everybody knew—their government guarantee—Fannie and Freddie had $1.73 trillion in debt outstanding. Of this, $520 billion had a maturity of less than one year. Of course, when a financial firm gets into trouble, the likelihood of creditors' rolling over their debt to new debt becomes small. Because one-third of their debt had maturities that were short-term in nature, their susceptibility to a massive run was quite high.

But this wasn't the *run* we most care about.

Instead, perhaps, it was the potential run on the banking system resulting from the banking sector's direct holdings of Fannie's and Freddie's debt. As described in section 4.1.1, the banking sector held 17% of Fannie Mae's and Freddie Mac's debt obligations outstanding. To the extent that large commercial banks—including Citigroup, Bank of America, JP Morgan Chase—also use wholesale short-term funding that is not insured, these banks were exposed to runs. And the problem was that no one knew which institutions were exposed to the 17% of Fannie's and Freddie's debt; so, from the perspective of creditors, the prudent action would be to withdraw funds, so as "to not be the mug left without savings."

But, believe it or not, this also wasn't the *run* we most care about.

The Federal Reserve's "Flow of Funds" data show that a large and increasing fraction of the agency debt is held by foreigners, often foreign central banks. Foreigners owned $492 billion in long-term U.S. agency debt in June 2002. This represented 10.8% of the outstanding amount. By June 2008, that number had almost tripled to$1.46 trillion, a 21.1% share. Irrespective of claims to the contrary by Treasury officials through the years, if foreign countries viewed Fannie Mae's and Freddie Mac's debt as de facto government debt—after all, what else does the term "government-sponsored enterprise" elicit?—then default on Fannie's and Freddie's debt would have consequences for confidence in the U.S. *sovereign* debt. In fact, the largest holders of agency debt are China and Japan. Given that these same foreign investors are holding two-thirds of U.S. Treasury debt as well, a default or even just a loss in valuation of agency debt would have enormous reputational effects for the U.S. Treasury, which could lead to a reduction in the foreigners' willingness to hold U.S. bonds in general. Given the fact that of the $5.21 trillion in U.S. Treasury debt outstanding in September 2008, a staggering $1.48 trillion were T-bills (i.e., less than one year in maturity), it is not inconceivable therefore that there could have been rollover risk in U.S. Treasuries. The result would be higher interest rates for everyone at the least and more likely a significant upheaval in global financial markets.

This *is* the run we care about.

As former treasury secretary Henry Paulson recounts in his book *On the Brink,* following the announcement in mid-July 2008 that the Treasury had acquired emergency powers to deal with Fannie's and Freddie's problems:

From the moment the GSEs' problem hit the news, Treasury had been getting nervous calls from officials of foreign countries that were invested heavily in Fannie and Freddie. These calls ratcheted up after the legislation (granting powers to the Treasury to put GSEs into conservatorship but also to extend unlimited support to them). Foreign investors held more than $1 trillion of the debt issued or guaranteed by the GSEs, with big shares held in Japan, China and Russia. To them, if we let Fannie or Freddie fail and their investments were wiped out, that would be no different from expropriation. They had bought these securities in the belief that the GSEs were backed by the U.S. government. They wanted to know if the United States would stand behind the implicit guarantee—and what this would imply for other U.S. obligations, such as Treasury bonds.[8]

Metaphorically, seeing foreign institutions and governments lining up outside the Board of Governors of the Federal Reserve System at 20th Street and Constitution Avenue in Washington, D.C., "to not be the mug left without savings," would spell an important moment in U.S. financial history and indeed globally, as it would mean the end of the greenback's status as the reserve currency of the world. There would be no turning back, no closing of Pandora's box.

Fannie and Freddie therefore were too big to fail; and, with everyone in private markets knowing this and many in government promoting them, Fannie and Freddie grew ever larger, with their debt effectively ending up being a significant fraction of the U.S. government debt.

4.1.4 Fire Sales

During the holiday season of 2008, Saks Fifth Avenue in New York City dropped 70% off the price on all of its luxury line of clothes. It was an unheard of practice to conduct fire sales before the Christmas holiday. Madison Avenue boutiques were in an uproar. Luxury designers were outraged. How could they sell $500 Manolo Blahnik shoes—the ones made famous in the *Sex in the City* television series—for just $150? Well, in the economy of the winter season of 2008–9, they were $150 shoes, and many Madison Avenue boutiques went under, literally, almost overnight. A walk down Madison Avenue in February 2009 would have shown one closed store after another.

And similarly this was the case for the illiquid securities held by the banking sector in the fall of 2008. Banks had gorged themselves on illiquid mortgage-backed securities that carried some possibility of default. For taking this liquidity and credit risk, they received a nice premium over their funding rate. And, in normal times, they pocketed it as profits. Now, in the economic crisis, it had come back to bite them, and the securities had become very impaired.

Why?

First, there is a price for liquidity—that is, people are willing to pay for the ability to convert securities into cash immediately. During the crisis, most investors were deciding between parking their cash in a Treasury money market fund that pays almost nothing or putting money under their mattress. The last thing that investors wanted was to own esoteric securities that they would have to hold to maturity because no one was willing to buy them. They might need cash at short notice and were paying for that privilege by earning zero interest.

Second, there was a growing possibility that the loans that were underlying these securities were going to default. In other words, the promised payments on these securities were less likely to be paid out. What was a security worth? The initial cost, or what one could sell it for? It would be great to pretend that a house was worth what someone paid for it in June 2006. But house prices in the fall of 2008 reflected not a temporary drop but a longer-term correction.

Of course, the problem was that Fannie Mae and Freddie Mac were the largest holders of relatively illiquid mortgages and mortgage-backed securities—in fact, $1.52 trillion worth as of September 2008. Within this portfolio, Fannie and Freddie (along with the FHLB System) held $308 billion of the ratings-inflated nonprime AAA MBS, which became notoriously difficult to value once the crisis started.

It is clear that the failure of the GSEs would have led to a fire sale of these assets that would infect the rest of the financial system, especially the banking sector and broker-dealers that were holding similar assets. To the extent that the MBS market is one of the largest debt markets, the fire sale could have brought other financial institutions down—similar to our analogy to Madison Avenue boutiques when Saks Fifth Avenue conducted its own version of a fire sale. What is worse, the rescue of Fannie and Freddie required the Treasury to be "in bed with the Fed," and any future resolution of these giants would also have to take into account the implications for the overexpanded Federal Reserve balance sheet.

5

END OF DAYS

In come the waves: The worldwide rise in
house prices is the biggest bubble in history.
Prepare for the economic pain when it pops.

—Economist, *June 16, 2005*

As of December 2007, five months after the financial crisis started but nine months before the financial system collapsed, the two largest government-sponsored enterprises (GSEs), Fannie Mae and Freddie Mac, looked quite different from how they did a decade earlier in 1997.

For example, in 1997, with $21 billion of shareholder equity, and a $481 billion portfolio of mortgages and $1.06 trillion of mortgage-backed security (MBS) guarantees, supported by $256 billion of notional financial derivatives, the combined two GSEs had a leverage ratio (i.e., dollar mortgage exposure/shareholder equity) of 72. As high as this leverage was, their mortgage exposure was fairly safe. Of the $481 billion portfolio, less than $10 billion was in private-label securities backed by the riskier nonprime mortgages. While data are sparser from this period, the analysis in chapter 2 showed that, in terms of guaranteeing riskier MBS in 1997, the GSEs had started to support risky loans with high loan-to-value ratios and low credit scores. But not only was this a small percentage of the risky issuance in 1997; it was also just a few years earlier that the two GSEs had even ventured into this arena.

Move forward 10 years to year-end 2007: Fannie and Freddie had essentially tripled in size—with $70.7 billion of shareholder equity, a $1.43 trillion mortgage portfolio, $3.50 trillion in MBS guarantees, and a much larger derivatives book of $2.26 trillion. The growth in the GSEs illustrated here, and described in detail in chapter 1, is astonishing in its own right. But the hidden fact underlying this growth, discussed in chapters 2 and 3, was the nature of this growth: Fannie's and Freddie's foray into riskier mortgage portfolios was now $313.7 billion, or 22%, compared to just 2% 10 years earlier. Their mortgage book as a percentage of MBS guarantees now included mortgages with FICO scores less than 660 (14%, or $498 billion), LTVs greater than 80% (17%, or $589 billion), and interest-only or negatively amortizing mortgages (6%, or $210 billion).

This was not your mother's GSE.

It has become a convenient excuse for Fannie and Freddie executives to blame their failure on the collapse in housing prices and the financial crisis in general. For example, Robert Levin, Fannie Mae's chief business officer and executive vice president during the period up to the crisis, wrote in testimony in April 2010 to the Financial Crisis Inquiry Commission: "This extraordinary upheaval in the mortgage market and the economy placed stresses on Fannie Mae that would have been difficult for the company to withstand regardless of any business decisions that preceded the crisis."

While there is no doubt that the massive drop in housing prices sealed Fannie's and Freddie's fates, their financial failures would have happened anyway even with a mild housing correction or economic downturn. And given their systemic risk as detailed in chapter 4, the financial system would have been put at risk even in milder times.

And, in the financial crisis of 2007–9, Fannie's and Freddie's effective bankruptcy was not a borderline failure in any way. For example, the Congressional Budget Office (CBO) estimates that total losses for the two GSEs could be on the order of $400 billion. It was not even close. The problem with Fannie and Freddie was their business model, and their incentives to ramp up risk on the taxpayer's dime, not the catastrophic drop in housing.

Nevertheless, it did not help that the worst financial and economic crisis in the United States since the Great Depression was preceded by a real estate boom of historic proportions. Households could get more debt than ever before by borrowing against the ever-increasing value of their homes. Mortgage lenders were in a race to the bottom in terms of the quality of the loans that they issued. This slippage of credit standards was in part because it had become commonplace for them to pass on the mortgage loans to others in the form of MBS and collateralized debt obligations (CDOs). Large, complex financial institutions had found ways to hold securitized assets on their balance sheets with little capital backing them.

Checks and balances down the securitization chain thus weakened. This allowed subprime mortgage lenders to pursue aggressive lending practices. A subtle effect of the subprime lending boom was that the share of higher quality—"conforming"—mortgages fell. As described in chapter 3, the GSEs gradually lost market share in the MBS market. To keep up profits for their shareholders, they started buying ever more risky mortgages in the years 2003 to 2007. The quality of their portfolio was not helped by Congress's mandate for Fannie and Freddie to buy an ever higher proportion of mortgages from low-income households and underserved areas.

Not long after house prices peaked in the summer of 2006, the first subprime mortgage lenders started to go belly-up. Bear Stearns' hedge funds collapsed in June 2007, primarily because of problems in their mortgage portfolio. In 2007 Freddie's and Fannie's gigantic portfolio of loans incurred $8 billion in credit losses, and the GSEs turned their first annual loss after 15 years of record profits. These credit losses spiraled out of control in the second half of 2008. Because the GSEs were so highly levered, any credit losses had a dramatic impact on their solvency. On September 7, 2008, the GSEs were placed in the government's conservatorship.

As of the late summer of 2010, the GSEs have used up $145 billion from their initial $200 billion government lifeline, with analysts projecting at least another couple of hundred billions to fill the hole of their credit losses from their misguided mortgage investments of 2007 and earlier. This bailout will have the largest net costs (outlays minus recoveries) of all of the government's bailout efforts, far exceeding the cost of the AIG bailout or the Troubled Asset Relief Program (TARP).

The GSE bailout represents the creation of a "bad" bank for mortgage-related losses in the United States. Through the conservatorship, the government has kept the mortgage market afloat in 2009 and 2010, and it has used the GSEs as a tool for mortgage modifications. This chapter relives the collapse in slow motion.

5.1 FALLING OFF A CLIFF

On March 1, 1984, NASA sent the fifth Landsat satellite into space. At an altitude of 450 miles, its purpose was to transmit pictures of Earth, taking about 16 days to cover its entirety. At the U.S. Geological Survey's center for Earth Resources Observation and Science, one can download these pictures over the past 25 years. Focusing on images of Las Vegas in 5-year intervals from 1984 to 2009, one can observe the remarkable growth of this city—its push toward the desert just west of Vegas in the 1980s, southward in the 1990s, and finally southwest by 2004. From a population of 741,000 in 1990 to 1,846,000 by the end of 2005, with a corresponding increase in housing units of 317,000 to 737,000, Las Vegas was the fastest growing metropolitan area in the United States.[1]

A case in point: leaving the Las Vegas strip, after just a few miles of driving on Interstate 15 on the way to Los Angeles, you will come to the "Blue Diamond Road" exit, which takes you west toward the mountains. Within five miles, you will run into what was at one point the fastest-growing master plan community in the United States: Mountain's Edge. Intended to hold 12,000-plus homes, along with a network of schools, professional offices, restaurants, and neighborhood shops, the community was a model for Las Vegas's growth. Development started in 2004, with home prices appreciating more than 50% per square foot in the following two and a half years.

Mountain's Edge outside of Las Vegas represented the sweet spot of the new business model of the GSEs. With median home values at $450,000, down payments as low as 8% still potentially qualified for the conforming mortgage limit of $417,000—the one rule that the GSEs were subject to without exception. While the LTV of 80% was also hard-wired, a little credit enhancement in terms of private mortgage insurance on top of the mortgage enabled the GSEs to securitize the mortgage. And then FICO scores below 660, or low documentation on the income front—well, that was between the regulator (OFHEO) and the GSEs. The GSEs were becoming just another nonprime mortgage lender.

By early 2008, Mountain's Edge of Las Vegas had become a poster child for the troubles of the housing market. With only two-thirds of the homes completed, mega-grocery stores half finished, and construction not yet begun on local parks, Mountain's Edge resembled other communities stretching from Stockton to Phoenix to Miami. At the peak of the crisis, in February 2009, 57 homes in the Mountain's Edge community were sold from the group of homes that had also been sold in 2006—the peak of the "housing bubble." The average drop in price for these homes was a staggering 48%. With homeowners' committing very little equity to the underlying values of these homes, almost all of these losses were borne by the creditors—the biggest of which were most likely the GSEs.

More broadly, national house prices peaked in the late spring of 2006. Since then, they have fallen back to levels not seen since 2003. Specifically, the 10-city Case-Shiller index fell from 227 in April 2006 to 152 in May 2009. The three-year 40% decline is by far the largest on record. The previous decline, which started in 1990, also lasted three years but was only 9% from peak to trough. The states of Nevada, California, Arizona, and Florida were especially hard hit. Las Vegas, Phoenix, Miami, and San Francisco saw declines of 60% or more. The Freddie Mac conventional mortgage house price index shows a more modest 17% nationwide decline. Relative to rents or median income, house prices returned back to their historical average.

Alongside the collapse in house prices, residential construction fell off a cliff: an 84% drop from the end of 2005 in residential investment. New housing permits went from 2 million units per year in 2002–6 to a historic low of 0.5 million in 2009. The collapse in residential investment, alongside the decline in consumption and business investment, plunged the U.S. economy into the worst postwar recession. Real GDP fell four consecutive quarters from mid-2008 to mid-2009. Between the official start of the recession in December 2007 and the end in June 2009, about 8 million jobs were lost. Macroeconomic risk, as measured by the VIX index or by the volatility of GDP, has returned with a vengeance after nearly 25 years of calm.

In the wake of falling house prices, new mortgage originations dropped sharply. Many of the largest private-label originators, such as Countrywide, either went out of business or were sold in distress to large commercial banks. Essentially the only new mortgages that were issued in the second half of 2008 and in 2009 were mortgages that could be bought by the GSEs or the FHA/VA. The PLS market was essentially dead in 2008 and 2009, accounting for less than 3% of MBS originations, down from 50% in 2006. Freddie's and Fannie's share in new mortgage originations increased back to 75% in 2009 (up from 30% in 2006), with the FHA accounting for 20% in 2009 (up from 3%

in 2006). In today's mortgage market, the government truly is the lender of last resort.

The final aspect of the bust was the tidal wave of foreclosures. The initial wave of foreclosures in 2007 and 2008 was tied to the interest rate resets on ARMs and on other exotic mortgages, such as option-adjusted ARMs. Such rate resets raised monthly payments at a time when refinancing was not an option because of falling property prices. However, as the economy entered into a full-force recession, increasing numbers of foreclosures came from people who lost their jobs. Foreclosures tend to follow job losses with a three- to six-month delay. In 2009, 2.8 million households received foreclosure filings, up 21% from 2008 and 120% from 2007.

5.2 THE COLLAPSE OF FREDDIE AND FANNIE, AND THE CONSERVATORSHIPS

5.2.1 Early Warning Signs

With nationwide housing markets collapsing, a deep recession, and an increasingly risky mortgage portfolio, the GSEs showed their first losses in 2007. The combined $5 billion loss was due to credit-related expenses of $8 billion.

In early July 2008, three months after the mortgage-related collapse of Bear Stearns and with the stock market down 20% from its peak, speculation was rampant that the government would have to rescue Freddie Mac and Fannie Mae—at least in terms of their obligations to their creditors. By then, the GSEs had already lost an enormous amount of stock market capitalization. In 2007 Freddie's share price fell by 50% from $64.00 to $32.00, while Fannie's stock lost 36% of its value. By July 1, 2008, Freddie's stock had dropped by another 50% to $16.00. Doubts about the future of the GSEs plunged Freddie's share price a further 50% to $7.70 on July 10. In the first week of September, the stock traded at $5.10. Fannie's share price dropped from $27 to $21 over the first half of 2008. Over the summer of 2008, it fell further to $12.60, just prior to the conservatorships. Clearly, the stock market anticipated much worse times to come for the GSEs as early as the fall of 2007. It started anticipating a rescue for creditors in June–July of 2008, with little residual value for equity holders. In all, $60 billion in market capitalization was lost between October 2007 and early September 2008.

Bond markets also spelled early signs of trouble. The difference in yield between the debt of five-year Fannie Mae debt and five-year Treasuries rose sharply from 0.2% per year at the end of 2006 to 0.4% in September 2007, and to 1.0% in September 2008. This increase in yields reduced the value of widely held GSE debt. In addition, the GSEs were forced to issue shorter-term bonds in the second half of 2008.

The cost of insuring against a default on the bonds issued by the GSEs also started to rise. The CDS spread for Fannie Mae was a low 6 basis points in December 2006 and rose to an all-time high of 88 basis points in March 2008. While noticeable, this 82-basis-point increase in CDS spreads pales in comparison to the 500-basis-point increase in the CDS spread for Bear Sterns or for Lehman Brothers just before the latter's bankruptcy. This difference reflects the market's belief that the government would likely bail out the bondholders of Fannie and Freddie but not the bondholders of the investment banks. Indeed, this belief turned out to be correct ex-post when Fannie and Freddie CDS contracts were settled at prices near par.

Ironically, although Fannie and Freddie were clearly getting close to extreme financial difficulties, their regulator FHFA could not do much about addressing their imminent troubles because the regulator's most recent semiannual regulatory exams had not cited capital shortfalls. The special private corporation status of these GSEs meant that the government—the Treasury—could inject capital into them, on terms that the GSEs agreed to, all while their debt had been perceived as being implicitly guaranteed by the government and while the GSEs had themselves taken full advantage of that perception to expand their balance sheets to unreachable heights in the context of private corporations.

5.2.2 First Rescue Attempts

Regulators and policy makers alike tried to assure the public that the GSEs were solvent while in the background they pieced together the emergency rights to take over Fannie and Freddie, even while the two enterprises remained publicly traded companies. Finally, in the wake of the collapsing stock prices, on July 13, 2008, Treasury Secretary Henry Paulson announced that he had obtained the "bazooka": a potential government bailout of unprecedented scale that would signal a confidence-boosting effort to backstop the GSEs in coordination with the Federal Reserve. The plan increased the line of credit that was available to the GSEs from the Treasury, established the right for the Treasury to purchase equity in the GSEs, and introduced a consultative role for the Federal Reserve in a reformed GSE regulatory system. On the same day, the Federal Reserve announced that the Federal Reserve Bank of New York would have the right to lend to the GSEs as necessary.

The Housing and Economic Recovery Act of 2008, signed into law on July 30, 2008, expanded regulatory authority over Fannie Mae and Freddie Mac by the newly established Federal Housing Financing Agency. It also gave the U.S. Treasury the authority to advance funds for the purpose of stabilizing Fannie Mae or Freddie Mac, limited only by the amount of debt that the entire federal government is permitted by law to commit to. The law raised the Treasury's debt ceiling by $800 billion, in anticipation of the potential need for the Treasury to have the flexibility to support Fannie Mae, Freddie Mac, or the Federal Home Loan Banks.

As late as August 2008, Freddie and Fannie claimed that they were solvent with *regulatory* capital of $37 and $47 billion, respectively. However, these numbers excluded "temporary" paper losses of $34 billion at Freddie and $11 billion at Fannie. These were booked as tax-deferred assets, having the perverse effect of inflating the assets instead of reducing them. What's more, the GSEs did not adequately write down values of guarantees that had deteriorated in quality because of downgrades of the private mortgage insurers that were providing them.

But the facts on the ground spelled trouble. Freddie and Fannie saw exponential growth in mortgage delinquencies on their retained portfolios, as well as in their guarantee books. At Fannie Mae, delinquency rates on mortgages rose from an all-time low of 0.45% in 2000 to 0.98% in 2007, before jumping to 2.42% in 2008. Delinquencies at Freddie were only slightly lower, rising from an all-time low of 0.39% in 1999 to 0.65% in 2007, before tripling to 1.72% in 2008. More than half of the delinquencies were concentrated in four states: California, Arizona, Nevada, and Florida.

As a result, the losses at Fannie grew from $2.2 billion in each of the first and second quarters of 2008 to $29.0 billion in the third quarter of 2008. Similarly, the losses at Freddie were only $1 billion in the first half of 2008 but ballooned to $25.3 billion in the third quarter of 2008. It was ultimately these exploding losses and the GSEs' inability to raise private capital that prompted the Treasury to put the GSEs into the FHFA's conservatorship on September 7, 2008. Their combined 2008 losses would come in at $109 billion.

Each consecutive vintage of loans performed worse. The outright default rates were 1.4% on loans issued in 2004, 2% on loans issued in 2005, 3.3% on loans issued in 2006, and 2.6% on loans issued in 2007. With many more mortgages of the terrible 2006, 2007, and 2008 vintages yet to fail, the government decided to step in. The only way to address their impending bankruptcy—without risking a disorderly liquidation—was for the Treasury to exercise the exceptional emergency right that it had acquired to take charge.

5.2.3 Conservatorships

The conservatorships—not receiverships (which carried the possible connotation of prompt liquidation, as well as an unwanted inclusion of the GSEs in the federal government's financial accounts)—provided Fannie and Freddie each with a commitment of $100 billion from the Treasury in return for the Treasury's receiving a 79.9% ownership stake and $1 billion of preferred stock with a 10% coupon rate. This rescue mostly wiped out the existing shareholders: GSEs' stock prices fell to pennies on the dollar following the announcement (and eventually stopped trading altogether on the New York Stock Exchange in June 2010). The conservatorships also fully protected the senior and subordinated debt and the mortgage-backed securities of the GSEs. The agreement also required the GSEs to reduce the size of their retained portfolios to $850 billion each by December 31, 2009, and to reduce those portfolios each year by 10% until they reach $250 billion each. The agreement capped the maximum outstanding debt of Fannie and Freddie at 110% of the asset limit. No limits were placed on the guarantee business. The CEOs of Freddie and Fannie were dismissed. They were surprised, expecting to receive a government capital injection on their own terms instead.

The GSEs suffered another year of massive losses in 2009: $94 billion. Delinquency rates more than doubled from 2.42% in 2008 to 5.38% in 2009 at Fannie and from 1.72% in 2008 to 3.87% in 2009 at Freddie. Losses continued in the first quarter of 2010: $11.5 billion at Fannie and $6.7 billion at Freddie, and another $20 billion was tapped from the government lifeline. The second quarter of 2010 was the twelfth consecutive quarter of losses at Fannie Mae. Its $1.5 billion loss will be made up by the taxpayer once again. Likewise, Freddie Mac will draw $1.8 billion from its Treasury lifeline to fill its second quarter hole. As of the writing of this book, Fannie has drawn $85.1 billion while Freddie has drawn $63.1 billion. That is $148.2 billion out of the original $200 billion limit. In return for these drawdowns, the GSEs have paid $12.8 billion in dividends to the U.S. Treasury to date.

In response to the massive losses, the Treasury first increased its commitment to $200 billion per company in May 2009. It then quietly removed the ceiling on the bailout altogether on Christmas Eve 2009, promising to make up any further negative net worth in 2010, 2011, and 2012. This effectively amounts to writing a blank check to the GSEs.

In May 2009, two other modifications were made to the conservatorship agreements. The $850 billion asset limit was raised for each GSE to $900 billion, and the debt limit was raised to 120% of the asset limit. It was clarified that the 10% annual reductions in the asset portfolio had to be calculated on the basis of the asset limit and not the actual asset position. For example, the December 31, 2010, limit on the portfolio of each GSE is $810 billion.

In the judgment of the Congressional Budget Office (CBO), the conservatorship and the large ownership stake of the U.S. Treasury made Fannie Mae and Freddie Mac part of the government. The implication is that their operations should be reflected in the federal budget. We return to this issue in the next chapter.[2] In a January 2010 report, the Congressional Budget Office estimates that the GSEs' bailout realistically added $291 billion to the federal deficit in 2009 and that it will add another $99 billion in 2010–19. The total bailout cost will very likely exceed the initial $200 billion commitment.

5.2.4 Additional Programs

Several additional programs were introduced as part of the GSE bailout. First, the Treasury can directly purchase Freddie and Fannie MBS. As of December 2009, it had purchased $221 billion worth (having made no purchases since). Second, the Federal Reserve embarked on a massive GSE MBS purchase program in January 2009. It made its last purchase on March 31, 2010, having fully exhausted its $1,250 billion target capacity.

Third, the Federal Reserve purchased $172 billion in agency debt, the debt issued by Freddie and Fannie, between December 2008 and March 2010. It has nearly exhausted its target capacity of $175 billion. The latter two programs are responsible for a *doubling* of the Federal Reserve's balance sheet.

With the conservatorship comes an important question: should the debt of the GSEs be consolidated with the federal debt? Because the U.S. government has only a 79.9% and not an 80% stake in the GSEs, it does not technically have to consolidate the GSEs' accounts into the federal budget. (It also does not have to assume the pension liabilities of the GSEs.) We believe that it should do so, because the GSEs are de facto backed by the full faith and credit of the U.S. government debt. However, that implies that the national debt as of July 2010 is not $8.7 trillion, but $10.3 trillion. In fact, the taxpayer is ultimately liable for the default risk on all $8.1 trillion of GSE debt and GSE-backed securities. (But, of course, the consolidation would also move the GSEs' assets into the federal government's accounts.)

5.3 ANEMIC RECOVERY

While the recession in the United States ended in the summer of 2009, the country's macroeconomic problems are far from over. The current recovery has seen anemic employment growth. The housing market has barely perked up. New residential construction and applications to build new homes hit rock bottom in July 2010. New home sales declined to the lowest level ever recorded in May 2010, since records began in 1963. House prices have recovered modestly from a low point of 152 to 161 in June 2010, according to the Case-Shiller 10-city index, but are facing continued headwinds from mounting foreclosures. The 930,000 foreclosure filings in the first quarter of 2010 were up 16% from a year earlier. An additional 895,500 notices were filed in the second quarter of 2010, up 1% from a year earlier. It seems that the number of loans that are entering delinquency is abating, but the number of loans moving through the foreclosure process is still increasing. Large inventories of unsold homes, which are around 10 months' worth of supply, further hamper house price recovery. The homeowner vacancy rate of 2.5% is much above the long-run average of 1.7%. Finally, the expiration of the $8,000 federal tax credit for home purchasers at the end of April 2010 caused sharp drops in construction activity and in builders' share prices.

Faced with these headwinds, the U.S. home ownership rate reverted to 66.9% in the second quarter of 2010, its lowest level since 1999. This means that all of the gains made during the housing boom have been negated. In the previous housing bust of the 1990s, it took four years for house prices to recover from the bottom to their previous peak. Given that the 1990s cycle was substantially milder than the current one, we doubt that house prices will return to anywhere near their 2006 peak before 2014.

One important factor that hampers recovery is household debt. Including credit card and other debt, households collectively owed more than 114% of GDP, or $16.4 trillion in the first quarter of 2008. That is 30% of GDP, or $9.4 trillion more than just 10 years earlier. This indebtedness makes households reluctant to spend, as they are repairing their balance sheets. Figure 5.1 shows the evolution of mortgage debt relative to GDP and relative to housing wealth since 1952. Figure 5.1 illustrates the increasing indebtedness of U.S. households and the erosion in the fraction of housing that they own free and clear. Corresponding to the rise in mortgage debt, home equity fell from 62% to 35% of aggregate housing wealth from the third quarter of 2005 to the first quarter of 2009. Despite a well-publicized uptick in the savings rate, mortgage debt has fallen only by 5% of GDP and overall debt by 6% of GDP. Households still owed $15.8 trillion in debt in the first quarter of 2010, $12.8 trillion of which is mortgage debt. If history is a guide, bringing the debt ratio back to its preboom level will take years, perhaps decades. It certainly does not bode well for personal consumption, and hence for GDP growth, in the near term.

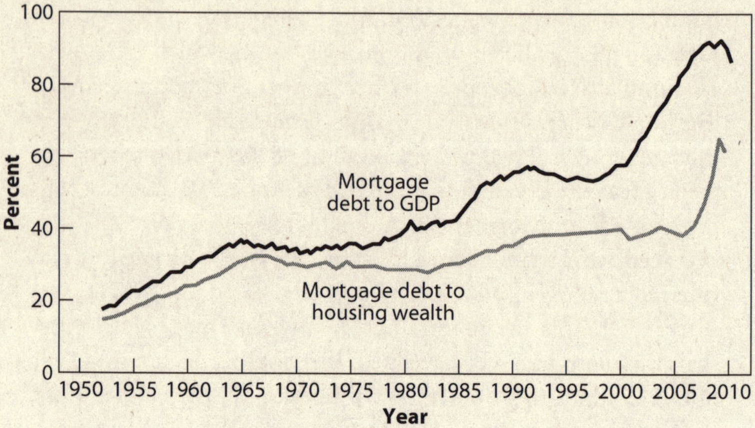

Figure 5.1: U.S. Mortgage Debt Relative to U.S. GDP and U.S. Housing Wealth. *Source:* Federal Reserve, Flow of Funds, Household sector's balance sheet

Given the state of the housing market, mortgage delinquencies at Freddie and Fannie are expected to rise in 2010 from their record levels in 2009. Mortgage delinquencies for single-family homes were 5.47% (4.99%) at Fannie and 4.13% (3.96%) at Freddie in the first quarter (second quarter) of 2010. As many as 11.3 million homeowners are currently "under water," and such negative equity position is associated with larger foreclosure rates. As a consequence of the many foreclosures, the GSEs have repossessed a large number of homes: 145,000 in 2009, up from 50,000 in 2007. Nationwide, foreclosure sales represented 29% of all house sales in 2009, up from 6% in 2007. Selling these houses in depressed housing markets, and alongside the repossessed properties of banks and thrifts, has led to losses as large as 40% of the value of the mortgage. Because the sales price of a foreclosed home is on average 27% below that of a comparable home not in foreclosure, these sales depress real estate prices and slow the recovery.

Mortgage modifications have become an important component of public interventions that are designed to reduce foreclosures. The GSEs are a key tool in this effort. In November 2008 to January 2009, the GSEs introduced a moratorium on foreclosures alongside private-sector lenders. The federal government's Home Affordable Modification Program (HAMP), started in April 2009, was targeted to help 3.2 million homeowners that were struggling. With efforts ramped up substantially in 2010, 1.3 million loans had received a trial HAMP modification and 0.4 million a permanent HAMP modification by the end of July 2010. In addition, another 0.5 million borrowers received a FHA loss mitigation intervention and 1.4 million a HOPE Now modification, for a total of 3.6 million government-subsidized modifications.

Some have argued that modifying mortgages is more difficult when these mortgages reside in securitization pools: win-win modifications do not take place, and loans are more likely to go into foreclosure when they are securitized.[3] Piskorski, Seru, and Vig find that loans that end up in banks' portfolios ultimately perform better than those held in securities, possibly because of an increased willingness by banks to offer modifications on loans of which they are the sole owners.[4] This argument would suggest a trade-off between the added liquidity of securitization and the ease of modification. A careful study by Hunt, however, finds no evidence of legal impediments on loan modifications.[5] This leaves open the possibility that it is not in the loan servicers' financial interest to pursue modifications, perhaps because banks are unwilling to recognize the low economic value of defaulted loans. What seems less controversial is the conclusion that, even when modification does take place, its success is often temporary. Using data on subprime mortgages that received modification between December 2005 and March 2009 (before the start of the HAMP program), a recent study shows a 56% re-default rate within 12 months of modification.[6] The success rate increases when the modification takes place through principal forgiveness rather than lower interest rates.

5.4 THE FEDERAL HOME LOAN BANK SYSTEM DURING THE CRISIS

The Federal Home Loan Bank System, the third GSE, which we have largely left out of our discussion so far, played a similar role to that of Freddie and Fannie. In particular, it proved to be a useful crisis management tool during the crisis, but it was used for purposes that are arguably beyond its mandate.

The financial crisis started in earnest in August 2007, when the $1.2 trillion asset-backed commercial paper (ABCP) market froze.[7] Investors were unwilling to renew the financing of the special purpose vehicles (SPVs) that housed the ABCP and the banks that set them up for fear that these banks were insolvent. With little or no access to other private market funding, the banks (through their SPVs) turned to the FHLB System. The FHLB System gives "advances" (loans) to commercial banks, thrifts, credit unions, and insurance companies that are the owner-members of the system. The advances are collateralized by residential mortgage-related assets, Agencies, and Treasuries.

During the second half of 2007, the FHLB System increased its advances (lending) to its members by $235 billion, to a total of $875 billion by the end of that year, a 36.7% increase.[8] In fact, the decline in the ABCP market is almost perfectly mirrored in the growth of the FHLB advances. Ten banks accounted for $150 billion of these advances. Washington Mutual, Bank of America, and Countrywide borrowed the largest amounts. As of June 30, 2008, advances stood at $914 billion. For comparison, the $1.3 trillion in total assets controlled by the FHLB System exceeded those for Fannie Mae or Freddie Mac at that time ($886 billion and $879 billion, respectively).

At the end of 2007 and in the first half of 2008, as Freddie's and Fannie's stock was being hammered for fear of insolvency, the FHLB System became guilty by association. Spreads on its bonds started to rise, and the cost of advances to its members rose as well. This made the FHLB System a less attractive funding facility for banks and thrifts, which turned to the Federal Reserve's discount window and new funding facilities instead. Indeed, the Fed's Term Auction Lending Facility (TALF) was set up in December 2007 and the Primary Dealer Credit Facility (PDCF) and Term Securities Lending Facility (TSLF) in March 2008. While the Federal Reserve is the lender of last resort, Ashcraft et al.[9] characterize the FHLB System as the *lender of next-to-last resort.*

5.5 FINAL THOUGHTS

This massive government support for the GSEs succeeded in shoring up the conforming housing market in 2009. This arguably prevented an even bigger collapse of U.S. housing and mortgage markets. Some mortgage-backed securities prices rallied in 2009, and mortgage interest rates were at an all-time low in the first half of 2010. While the GSEs (including the FHLB System) have proved to be a convenient recession-fighting tool, chapter 6 argues that the involvement of the Fed balance sheet in employing this tool has raised serious issues about conflicts of interest between fiscal and monetary policy, and chapter 8 makes a case that the recession-fighting advantage does not outweigh the costs of having large, systemically risky institutions that are trying to accomplish too many goals at once. We believe that the U.S. economy would ultimately be better served by breaking up the various functions of the GSEs.

In a fundamental sense, the critics of the GSEs were right: they were a problem. The specific quasi-public/quasi-private structure of the GSEs created incentives for excessive risk taking, at the ultimate expense of the tax-paying public; and having them around in mortgage markets made it convenient for each successive presidential administration to employ them for boosting short-run consumption and spending that was centered on housing, at the expense of some future administration and again ultimately the taxpayer. The confluence of these two distortions meant that over time, the GSEs morphed into the world's largest and most leveraged hedge funds, except that only they had government backing.

In the end, the GSEs had inadequate capital for the risks that they were taking. But virtually all critics got the immediate source of the problem wrong. What caused the financial downfall of the GSEs was not the interest rate risk embedded in their portfolios. Instead, the immediate source of the problem was the *credit risk* that stemmed from the poor quality of mortgages and investments that they took on and guaranteed in the middle of the decade. When the housing market crashed in the United States, this credit risk materialized and generated the large losses that wiped out the inadequate capital that they had maintained.

The force that led to the downfall of the GSEs is not uncommon to economic theory, which would call it a classic "race to the bottom" in bank risk-taking or underwriting standards. The important point is that the GSEs contributed to—and were influenced by—the risk taking of private financial firms that were competing with them in the same mortgage markets. In effect, a set of privileged institutions—Fannie and Freddie, backed by government guarantees and enjoying a lower cost of funding—entered a financial market (that of less-than-prime mortgages) hitherto operated by less-privileged institutions (mortgage banks, commercial banks, and investment banks, among others); the less-privileged institutions tried to guard against the entry by lending more aggressively, which prompted the more privileged to respond with aggression too. The subprime mortgage mess was in part due to government guarantees for Fannie and Freddie that distorted a level playing field, resulting in the debacle of mortgage finance.

6

IN BED WITH THE FED

Policy, whether it be printing money, guarantees or deficit spending, can prop up asset values for a while. This may even be useful in a liquidity crisis. But a solvency crisis is another thing. The longer policy distorts markets by ignoring fundamentals, the longer those reliant on market signals will sit on their hands. The Fed's recent decision to continue asset purchases shows there is no exit once this path is chosen. As we approach the second anniversary of the Fannie and Freddie bailouts, are we better off?

James Rickards (writer, economist, lawyer, and investment adviser), Financial Times, *August 12, 2010*

The financial crisis that started in the second half of 2007 highlighted the extraordinary power of the Federal Reserve (Fed) to intervene in the economy in a crisis. The title of the book by David Wessel, *In Fed We Trust: Ben Bernanke's War on the Great Panic*, sums it all up. Wherever there was a fire, the Fed used all its might to extinguish it. It also gave ammunition to those around the fire to defend themselves. In essence, the Fed played with flourish its role as the lender of last resort (LOLR)—lending to the financial sector (and even markets at large) when no one else would, so as to ensure the financial sector's stability. The Fed pumped liquidity into the system with creativity and expedience seen never before from any other central bank.

Macroeconomists who had long focused on the Fed's role of determining interest rates to ensure price stability and full employment found the Fed's methods "unconventional." But to economic historians, what the Fed attempted to do in this crisis was not that unconventional.[1] For example, in the panic of 1907, John Pierpont Morgan was asked to play the role of distributing Treasury's liquidity injection to the defaulting trust companies. This panic and the LOLR function played by Morgan were the origin of the Federal Reserve. But the absence of major financial crises in the United States since the Banking Act of 1933 placed this function in the background. The Fed's sole purpose was perceived to be price stability and full employment. There was, however, something unconventional about the Fed's LOLR activities in the current crisis: because of a lack of adequate authority and infrastructure for resolving the distress of government-sponsored enterprises (GSEs) and large and complex financial institutions, there seemed to be no tool at work other than the Fed's liquidity injections to get a handle on the crisis.

As David Wessel warns in his book, however, the Fed's war on the great panic is far from over. The Fed has still to mop up the liquidity that it has sprinkled all around.

The popular view is that the most important excursions of the Fed were in dealing with the failures of Bear Stearns and AIG. Contrary to this view, we will explain in this chapter that the Fed's biggest role in the crisis has been in dealing with the mortgage mess that was left by the collapse of Fannie Mae and Freddie Mac. In fact, since the start of their conservatorships in September 2008, these GSEs have been operating similarly to what a "bad bank" typically looks like at the end of a financial crisis. By buying more than $1.4 trillion worth of GSE debt and GSE-backed securities, the Fed has propped up the value of these bad banks' securities and the housing market more generally.

This massive foray of the Fed into the mortgage market, even if unavoidable in its war on the great panic, raises serious issues about how and when the Fed can retrench from the expansion. This may also curtail its freedom to raise interest rates and mop up the liquidity that it has injected in the economy. Ironically, we will argue, the more that the Fed gets caught up in the rest of the federal government's expansion into mortgage finance, the more likely it is that its future monetary policy will *not* be independent and will be largely driven by the need to monetize government debt.

We provide some suggestions for unwinding by the Fed, which ultimately needs a restart of the private mortgage markets (for which we propose reforms in chapter 8). We also discuss whether the special status that is enjoyed by the GSEs in various Federal Reserve operations—in normal times and in emergency—is desirable and how to restrict or eliminate this special status so that the Fed can avoid its current dilemmas in the future.

6.1 PUTTING OUT THE FIRES

As described in chapter 4, on July 13, 2008, Treasury Secretary Henry Paulson announced an effort to backstop ("conserve") the GSEs, in coordination with the Federal Reserve. Besides the direct support from the Treasury through a line of credit and ownership of Fannie's and Freddie's equity, the September 7, 2008, conservatorship plan introduced a consultative role for the Fed in a reformed GSE regulatory system. The same day, the Fed announced that it would have the right to lend to the GSEs as necessary. Effectively, the Fed was to be the lender of last resort not just to the private financial sector but also to the GSEs.[2]

Figure 6.1 shows the evolution of the Federal Reserve's balance sheet. It shows the dramatic rise in total securities that were held outright by the Fed, as well as the rise in two of its components: agency debt and mortgage-related assets, with the remainder being Treasuries held by the Fed. The Fed originally announced that it would purchase up to $100 billion in debt from

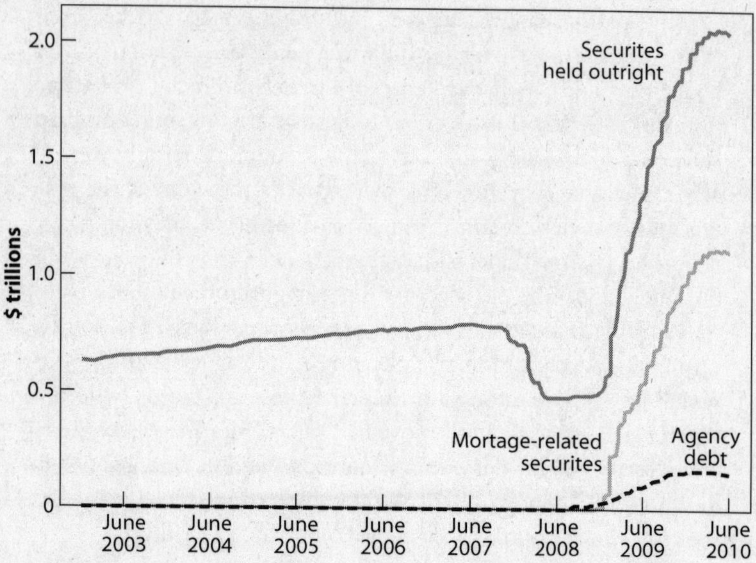

Figure 6.1: Securities Holdings of the Federal Reserve. *Source:* Federal Reserve Statistical Release (table 3, Factors supplying reserve balances: Detail for securities held outright); all numbers in trillions of dollars

Fannie Mae, Freddie Mac, and Federal Home Loan Banks, and up to $500 billion in mortgage-backed securities (MBS) issued by Fannie Mae, Freddie Mac, and Ginnie Mae. The Fed embarked on its massive purchase program in January 2009. But on March 18, 2009, it raised its intended purchases of agency debt to $200 billion (a $100 billion increase) and of agency MBS to $1,250 billion (a $750 billion increase). It made its last MBS purchase on March 31, 2010, having fully exhausted its $1,250 billion target capacity. It also purchased $172 billion in Freddie and Fannie debt, between December 2008 and March 2010.

Though we used the terms "last purchase" and "capacity," the Fed actually has discretion over the size and composition of its balance sheet. With regard to the composition of its balance sheet, the Federal Reserve Act (FRA) of 1913 limits the range of assets that the Fed may acquire directly. This range is considerably narrower than the range of assets that the Fed may accept as collateral in lending to eligible financial institutions, but the current range under FRA includes market debt and securities issued by the GSEs.[3] In essence, the Fed has substantial flexibility in expanding its interventions in GSE-related mortgages, and it has employed this flexibility by engaging in substantial purchases of the same.

These purchases by the Fed have amounted to about 8% of the economy's gross domestic product (GDP) and have become a central instrument of its "quantitative easing" monetary policy. The Bank of England followed a similar policy in the United Kingdom. Through these purchases, as well as massive purchases of Treasury debt, the Fed has kept long-term Treasury and mortgage rates historically low. The basic idea behind quantitative easing is that by reducing the supply of a set of securities floating around in the economy, the central bank can raise their prices, making those securities more attractive for investors to hold. The rise in prices can relax investors' financing constraints, allowing them to hold with ease other assets as well—for example, corporate bonds—and in turn raise their prices too.[4] In August 2010, the Fed announced its intention to avoid any "passive" unwinding of this program by purchasing Treasury debt with the moneys that become available as its MBS portfolio matures as a result of normal repayments and prepayments. Chairman Bernanke also offered further quantitative easing as its preferred intervention tool in case the Federal Reserve needed to stimulate the United States economy further (given that nominal interest rates are at the "zero bound").

The purchases have more than doubled the Federal Reserve's balance sheet from August 2007 to August 2010. They are an order of magnitude larger than the Fed's involvement in the rescues of Bear Stearns, AIG, and Citigroup. To provide a perspective: the Fed owns in its "Maiden Lane" portfolios $80 billion in assets ($30 billion from Bear Stearns and $50 billion from AIG), and it has guaranteed $306 billion of Citigroup's assets and $118 billion of Bank of America's. Taking account of the various first-loss pieces that were retained by the rescued institutions (or by JPMorgan Chase in the case of Bear Stearns) and some additional risk sharing in the cases of Citigroup and Bank of America, the Fed's net maximum exposure is around $420 billion, of which only $74 billion is on balance sheet—that is, purchased in exchange for reserves. While the public ire against the Fed is driven by its actions taken with respect to these private firms, the Fed's involvement here has been relatively small compared to the role that its balance sheet is playing for the GSEs.

In addition to direct purchases of Agencies and GSE-backed MBS, the Fed supported mortgage markets by setting up various emergency liquidity facilities. The Term Securities Lending Facility (TSLF) and the Primary Dealer Credit Facility, set up in March 2008, lent money to primary dealers, accepting Agencies and MBS as collateral. In September 2008 the Fed added the Asset-Backed Commercial Paper Money Market Mutual Fund Liquidity Facility, which advanced short-term funding to banks—again collateralized mostly by mortgage assets. At their peak, these three facilities provided $350 billion in advances. They were wound down in January 2009, whereas the direct purchases remain on the Fed balance sheet.

6.2 WHY INVOLVE THE FED?

It is true that the GSEs were simply too big to fail (as we have explained in chapter 4). In the midst of the financial crisis, they had to be bailed out, at least temporarily. To do so, the Treasury could have set up a special receivership, like the Resolution Trust Corporation (RTC) that was established after the savings and loan crisis in 1989. Why, instead, did the Fed balance sheet get involved so heavily?

While the GSE situation was originally meant to be dealt with as a receivership (like a chapter 7 bankruptcy liquidation), the financial market conditions in the summer of 2008 made it clear that they would need—at least temporarily—conservatorships (more like a chapter 11 bankruptcy in which the bankrupt firm can continue in business). While no serious attempt was made to liquidate any of the GSEs' holdings, to be fair, the Treasury was concerned that this would just not work. It did attempt in the fall of 2008 to launch a Troubled Asset Relief Program to purchase the distressed real estate assets on the banks' balance sheets. The plan to purchase—and eventually sell—the troubled assets lacked clarity and was later converted into a program that recapitalized bank holding companies against the purchase of senior preferred shares by the Treasury. A later attempt in March 2009 to launch a public-private investment program (PPIP) to purchase toxic assets from banks' balance sheets also met with only mild success. But the six-month period after the collapse of Lehman Brothers was hardly the time to liquidate assets or hope to succeed in attracting huge pools of new capital for buying U.S. mortgage risk.

A better plan would have been to combine the receivership and the *temporary* conservatorship ideas more directly, by employing an RTC-style asset management company that would warehouse the troubled mortgage assets of the GSEs (and other failed or troubled private financial firms that had to be rescued). The company should have been *prefunded* with a capital injection from the Treasury to weather the initial losses but charged with the mandate of eventually—not immediately—liquidating these assets into markets through public-private partnerships of the type that was employed by the RTC. We provide more detail of such a GSE RTC in chapter 8.

However, with the GSE collapse and the TARP funds unavailable for troubled mortgage purchases, the solution adopted was for the Fed's balance sheet to house the GSE assets and some of its debt. In the meantime, bank holding companies (backed through government-insured deposits in their bank subsidiaries and FDIC's loan guarantee programs) and the GSEs continued to expand their holdings of mortgage assets.[5] In effect, a massive transfer of mortgage-related assets took place toward those financial institutions that had the greatest access to government guarantees.

There is no shortage of proximate causes for why the Fed was so involved in the GSE bailout. A polarized U.S. Congress made it difficult formally to set up a RTC-style vehicle, leaving the Fed as the politically easiest way out. The Fed represented the most sophisticated regulatory agency around to handle the task with expediency. The Fed had already been dealing with the rescue of other large financial institutions and their mortgage portfolios. The Federal Reserve Act explicitly allows the Fed to engage in purchases of GSE debt and securities. Finally, as we detailed in chapter 1, the Federal Housing Enterprises Financial Safety and Soundness Act (FHEFSSA) of 1992, as well as some of the earlier pieces of legislation set in 1954, had laid out the special features of the GSEs. Most of these were reaffirmed by the Housing and Economic Recovery Act (HERA) of 2008, including the special status that the GSEs can use the Fed as their fiscal agent.

But the real question is why the Fed balance sheet continues to remain the place for holding GSE securities two years after the conservatorship of Fannie and Freddie. It has certainly been beyond what would seem to be a period of expediency in which the Fed support might have been necessary. To us, the answer lies in the government's unwillingness to recognize the GSE securities and debt on its own balance sheet. The Fed says that the mortgages are guaranteed by the Treasury; the Treasury refuses explicitly to recognize agency debt or mortgages on its balance sheet; and in the meantime the financial sector and foreign governments treat these securities as virtually riskless. Given their too-big-to-fail and interconnected-to-the-max status, it is simply incredible that the advantage of keeping the GSEs off balance sheet is for the government to have the flexibility to default on its debt if necessary. Any hint of such default would most likely trigger a run on a large number of domestic financial institutions, forcing the government to announce a complete bailout. The reserve status of the U.S. dollar could be substantially impaired. The government's credit risk spreads would shoot up overnight, as they did for Ireland in the fall of 2008 when it announced universal deposit insurance for its entire banking sector.

The real accounting trick in keeping GSE securities on the Fed balance sheet is the same as the one that underlay why Fannie Mae was privatized in 1968 in the first place: to keep its assets and liabilities unfunded from the current presidential administration's standpoint. Each administration grows the GSE guarantees, passing on ever more risks to the next one and to future taxpayers, without having to discipline current spending and without having to raise taxes in its own term of office to reduce fiscal imbalance. This policy creates fictional housing wealth that allows households to consume beyond their true borrowing capacity. Indeed, U.S. mortgage equity withdrawals were the engine of world economic growth between 2000 and 2007, but they could not be sustained once the housing bubble burst.

While this game of kicking the GSE can down the road has been ongoing for decades, the dire fiscal situation of the United States shines a new light on it. It amounts to a massive government gamble on the housing market. Despite their insolvency, Fannie's and Freddie's balance sheets continue to expand, and the government simply continues to plug the hole as and when losses arise. These losses—almost entirely due to the delayed recognition of the disastrous mortgage investments before 2008—have currently accumulated to $148.2 billion. The initial "keepwells" of $100 billion each for Fannie and Freddie have been raised to an unlimited draw on the Treasury through 2012. Instead of setting aside additional capital upfront for future losses, the cap on the size of the GSEs has been abolished. This is unlike Citigroup, another institution that would have hit insolvency without the Federal Reserve backstop and government recapitalization, but which is trying to shrink over time to about half of its precrisis size.

Continuing expansion of the Fannie and Freddie balance sheets and the current 70%+ share in guaranteeing new mortgages (more than 90% if we include FHA)—even as their risks remain unrecognized on the federal balance sheet—is the government's "doubling up" strategy. Doubling up is a strategy that financial traders follow when they have exhausted all of their capital in bets that have gone bad. Sound strategies might involve cutting the losses and exiting the trade, or raising more capital to withstand further losses. But these strategies would be privately costly for the traders. Hence, they either stay the course, hoping that things don't get worse, or even try to gamble more in the hope that they get resurrected before the losses materialize. In the case of the GSEs, such gambling takes the form of an undercapitalized expansion of their balance sheets. This is at least in part enabled by access to the Fed's balance sheet because this keeps risks temporarily off the government's balance sheet—that is, by leaving it for some future administration's balance sheet. It is possible that the gamble will pay off and the housing price rebound will eventually win the race against further losses on GSE mortgages, limiting future holes to be plugged. But the outcome of that race looks increasingly uncertain.

In summary, it is unclear why the Fed is the right choice as a long-term storage facility for GSE securities. This is really the task of an asset-management company. Even the Fed's holdings of securities from Bear Stearns and AIG are being "run" by an asset management firm for a fee. All of this can be transparently done through an RTC-style "bad bank" that is owned and funded by the Treasury. For now, however, things remain rather murky. The mingling of the Fed in the government's quasi-fiscal actions ("quasi" only because it involves off-balance-sheet debt and risks) has raised some difficult questions for the Fed's other roles, to which we turn next.

6.3 TO RAISE OR NOT TO RAISE

A principal conflict that has arisen with the Fed's ownership of GSE securities concerns whether the Fed's incentives will be well aligned with the economy's long-term growth and inflation prospects when it comes to raising interest rates. At least two issues are worth considering.

First, even though GSE securities and debt are effectively guaranteed by the U.S. government, carrying them on the Fed's balance sheet entails market risk due to changes in interest rates and prepayments. Suppose from the standpoint of price stability that it is desirable for the Fed to raise interest rates. Doing so would hurt the value of securities on its balance sheet. What would the Fed do? Would it err on the side of letting inflation build up? One could argue that someone has to bear the interest rate risk of these mortgages when rates rise. Why can't the Fed just take the losses? The issue, however, gets tricky when one considers the likely public and political perception of significant losses on the Fed balance sheet, especially given the criticism that its extravagant role in the crisis has already invited. The current decision makers at the Fed might feel somewhat caught up in their past decisions—much as corporate boards do in biting the bullet and firing an incompetent CEO whom they themselves hired.

Second, the reason why the Fed has felt comfortable buying GSE securities and continuing with purchases of Treasuries is that banks mostly leave the swapped reserves ("money") in accounts that they maintain with the Fed. Since October 2008 (expedited from the originally planned 2011 date), the Fed has been paying interest on reserves that banks maintain with it. Paying interest on reserves has ensured that even though the Fed created and used the reserves to purchase securities, they are not floating around in the economy, multiplying the quantity of financial transactions and running the risk of triggering inflation. When the Fed raises interest rates, it will have to pay more on these reserves. If the Fed has not been able to sell the securities on its balance sheet into markets, then the additional reserves would also have to be paid higher interest rates in order to ensure that banks keep them deposited at the Fed and out of circulation. Again, the Fed's decision to raise interest rates would be less complex without the additional reserves that were created to purchase GSE securities.

Given the weak state of the U.S. economy's recovery (as of August 2010), there seems to be little inflation risk in the short run. Real household spending is growing at an annual rate of only 1–2%, household savings have gone up to 6% of disposable income, corporations are sitting on piles of cash, and banks' lending standards to households and small businesses remain tight. If anything, the main worry seems to be one of a further decline in aggregate demand and price deflation. What is the big deal if in a jobless environment with deflationary risk, such as the one we are in, the Fed is constrained somewhat in its interest rate decisions?

This is, however, a massive problem for the future. Because interest rates are *the* most important prices to be set in the economy, any systematic error in interest rate policy can distort capital allocation and lead to asset price bubbles. Banks and corporations are both sitting on a lot of cash. Guided by the invisible hand of low interest rates, they might start deploying the cash for investments, and collectively build a heap of overinvestment, only to fall off the overinvestment precipice eventually. In fact, the housing boom until 2006 also fed off low interest rates for many years. Yes, we do not have significant lending and investments happening now, but when the pendulum swings back to growth, will the Fed balance sheet be in shape to correct the stimulus-induced investment boom and inflation, and to do so in a timely fashion? Without doubt, traditional monetary policy would be much more straightforward without more than a trillion dollars worth of interest-rate-sensitive assets on the Fed's balance sheet.

Narayana Kocherlakota, president of the Federal Reserve Bank of Minneapolis, said in a recent speech that the bank's estimations suggest that even 20 years out, the Fed is likely to have approximately $250 billion of MBS holdings.[6] This is because any unwinding of the MBS must be done sufficiently slowly to avoid a significant price impact. At present, attempts to unwind the securities in large chunks are likely to be met by anemic private demand. Hence, the Fed's holdings of MBS, Agencies, and Treasuries will likely remain above $1 trillion one to two years hence, when interest rates may need to be raised again. This quandary over raising rates creates undesirable regulatory uncertainty.

6.4 THE DODD-FRANK ACT, THE FED, AND FANNIE-FREDDIE

The fallout for the Fed from its emergency actions in dealing with the failures of Bear Stearns and, in particular, AIG has not exactly been friendly. For instance, Congressman Ron Paul wanted to *End the Fed* in his bestselling book with that title and in a more softened form in the Grayson-Paul amendment that was introduced in 2009, which would have subjected Fed decision making to audits and second-guessing by Congress. Somewhat fortunately, the Dodd-Frank Act of 2010, the biggest overhaul of financial regulation in the United States since the 1930s, mutes the Paul proposals.

However, the Fed's actions that pertain to agency debt and securities have remained relatively unquestioned in the government debates. As explained, this is in fact what the government wants. In contrast, the Fed's ability to provide emergency lending or support to individual financial firms—other than depository banks—is being restricted by the Dodd-Frank Act. Specifically, the Dodd-Frank Act legislates that emergency lending by the Federal Reserve can no longer be provided to any "individual, partnership, or corporation" but only to "participant[s] in any program or facility with broad-based eligibility."[7] Second, the act states that "any emergency lending program or facility is for the purpose of providing liquidity to the financial system, and not to aid a failing financial company, and that the security for emergency loans is sufficient to protect taxpayers from losses and that any such program is terminated in a timely and orderly fashion." The goal of these restrictions is presumably to reduce the moral hazard of too-big-to-fail nonbanks and to prevent taxpayer assistance for their restructuring or liquidation (which under other parts of the Dodd-Frank Act is proposed to be driven through the new FDIC-led resolution mechanism).

However, Dodd-Frank places no such *explicit* restrictions on the Fed with respect to lending to the GSEs and purchasing their debt and securities, even though they are technically nonbanks. While there is some legal ambiguity on this matter, we conjecture that the GSEs will continue to have full access to the Fed under the new legislation. Explicitly imposing any restrictions with regard to Fed purchases of GSE debt and securities would in fact involve amending the Federal Reserve Act. It is worth reconsidering whether some restrictions might be desirable.

There is little economic reason why the Fed's lender of last resort (LOLR) role should distinguish between a nonbank and a GSE if both pose an identical systemic threat and moral hazard problem. Indeed, while the systemic threat is certainly greater with the GSEs, there is in fact a much bigger moral hazard problem too as a result of their unfettered access to government guarantees.

When the central bank of a country is, by legislation, required to support government-sponsored enterprises, but such support is clearly ruled out for others, what is created is a serious lack of a level playing field in the financial sector. As we explained in chapter 3, this situation can only lead to a race to the bottom in financial risk taking. Eventually, the government institutions will be bailed out more generously and will crowd out the private firms, as we are seeing now in mortgage markets. Besides, the central bank may not have much independence precisely when it is most necessary, such as in a severe financial crisis.

The reforms that are required to address this predicament raise questions that go to the very roots of government involvement in finance and to what extent such involvement should be accorded a special status. But we think such reforms are necessary.

We recommend that there be a preauthorized standby authority—for example, a specially designated liquidity facility—in the

Treasury Department. This facility should be limited in scale and prefunded by the government budget. It should support any marketwide purchases of securities by the Fed when an emergency need arises in a crisis. That is, the Fed will merely be the agent that is executing the liquidity support, but there will already be funding that is present for all of these purchases. This funding would buy back the collateral from the Fed within a prespecified period—say, 6 to 12 months. The Fed cannot hold these assets on its balance sheet for long. Such an arrangement would mitigate the inevitable conflict between requiring quasi-fiscal actions by the central bank and securing its independence, while allowing for a timely crisis response.

Unfortunately, nothing in the Dodd-Frank Act directly addresses the confounding of fiscal and monetary policy roles of the Fed that we have witnessed in the continuing resolution of the crisis.

6.5 SUMMARY

In times like these, one cannot escape the thought that the Fed will ultimately have to inflate away government debt if the Treasury does not cut back soon on spending or raise taxes. In other words, rather than the Fed using its monetary policy tool kit to anchor inflation expectations, these will be set by the government's debt or fiscal policy. The Fed will be printing money and setting interest rates to target the value of government debt.[8] When monetary policy and fiscal policy in the economy get so intertwined, what exactly is meant by the independence of the Fed? Most economists would, however, want the Fed's decision-making powers to remain independent and focused on the economy's long-term growth and price stability objectives. Bringing the GSE debt and risks explicitly into government budget planning will most likely lead to restrictions on their growth and reductions in the fiscal deficit. It would also make it more likely that the Fed's monetary policy remains independent in the future. If needed, the Treasury should set up a separate and prefunded "bad bank" for difficult GSE assets with the sole task of liquidating them over time in private markets.

Given the Fed's multiple roles in attempts to resolve the crisis, the Federal Reserve governor Ben Bernanke has been calling on the Congress for an action plan on the reforms at least since February of 2010: *"The sooner you get some clarity about where the ultimate objective is, the better."*[9]

For now, the worry is that, just like Fannie and Freddie, the Fed too is being asked—or required—by the government to perform too many roles, often conflicting ones. We know how this ended up for Fannie and Freddie. It should not happen to the Fed.

7

HOW OTHERS DO IT

> The U.S. economy, once the envy of the world, is now viewed across the globe with suspicion. America has become shackled by an immovable mountain of debt that endangers its prosperity and threatens to bring the rest of the world economy crashing down with it. The ongoing *sub-prime* mortgage crisis, a result of irresponsible lending policies designed to generate commissions for unscrupulous brokers, presages far deeper problems in a U.S. economy that is beginning to resemble a giant smoke-and-mirrors Ponzi scheme. And this has not been lost on the rest of the world.
>
> —*Hamid Varzi, "A Debt Culture Gone Awry,"* International Herald Tribune, *August 17, 2007*

While countries organize their housing and mortgage markets quite differently across the globe, very few have the level of government support for home ownership of the United States. Indeed, none have institutions quite like Fannie Mae and Freddie Mac (and the extensive apparatus of other government-sponsored enterprises). This makes other countries interesting cases to study when considering a radical overhaul of the United

States' housing finance system. Is a high level of government participation in mortgage markets necessary?

An important conclusion is that many countries with less government involvement in housing finance institutions, when compared to the U.S. experience, have comparable home ownership rates and comparably affordable housing. It also is the case that the extensive government intervention in housing markets in the United States has not helped avoid a large drop in mortgage market activity and in house prices during 2006–10. In fact, house prices fell by less and the rebound was stronger almost everywhere else, with the exception of Ireland and Spain.

It is indeed paradoxical that the country with the most vibrant private market for raising equity has the greatest government presence in mortgage-related fixed-income markets. But this may precisely be the reason that its equity markets have remained relatively robust to the Great Recession, but that the mortgage markets continue to remain moribund in spite of the (even) greater government presence than in the past.

7.1 HOUSING FINANCE INSTITUTIONS AND HOME OWNERSHIP ACROSS THE GLOBE

Housing finance differs markedly across the world along several dimensions. Differences exist in funding, the range of mortgage products and markets, government support, home ownership rates, and bankruptcy legislation.

7.1.1 Who Funds Mortgage Credit?

There are three major funding models for mortgage credit in developed economies. The first one is the deposit-based system, where banks originate mortgages funded by deposits and hold the mortgages on their books. Figure 7.1 shows that this "old model of banking" is still the dominant type of mortgage

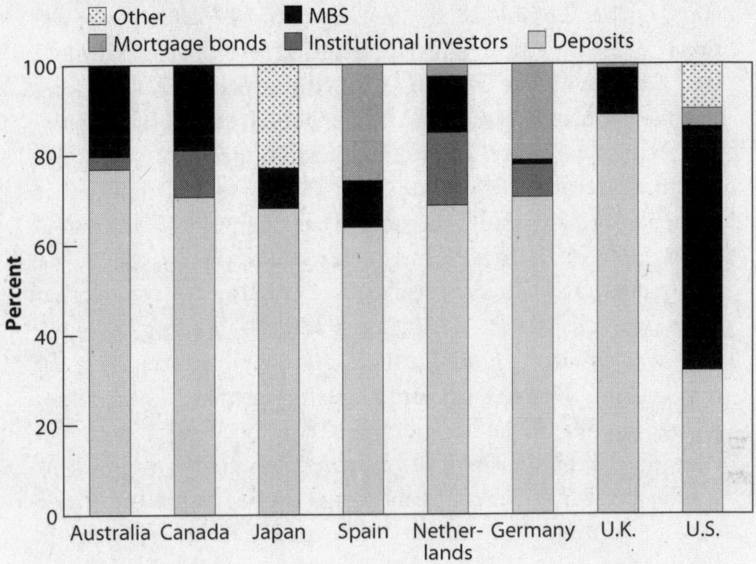

Figure 7.1: Mortgage Funding in Various Countries. *Source:* Canada Mortgage Bonds Program Evaluation, Final report, Prepared by KPMG LLP, June 2008.

finance in most countries outside the United States. The benefit of this system is that the lender retains the risk of mortgages and has appropriate incentives at the time of origination. The cost, as generally argued, is that this originate-to-hold model renders mortgages illiquid and limits mortgage funding to the supply of deposits and other liabilities that are issued by banks and other depository institutions. Also, if the depository institutions originate and hold fixed-rate mortgages, they are likely to be plagued by the interest rate risk that engulfed the U.S. savings and loan industry three decades ago.

The second type is the "new model of banking," where loans are no longer held on banks' balance sheets, but are originated to distribute in the form of mortgage-backed securities (MBS). Figure 7.1 shows that, as of 2005–6, the United States had the largest securitization share (higher than 50% of all originations), while no other country exceeded 25%. Only Australia and Canada have sizable MBS markets. The new model of banking became popular as a way of providing liquidity to mortgage markets, but it has always been questioned on incentive grounds—specifically, that the "originate-to-distribute" model implies that original mortgage lenders do not have enough "skin in the game" to originate well. More recently, as a result of the financial crisis, researchers have added to the chorus of criticisms by arguing that this new model is more fragile than traditional banking and more subject to regulatory arbitrage (i.e., exploiting loopholes in capital requirements between different regulatory regimes).[1] Difficulties of loan modifications for mortgages that are in default are yet another recent criticism of the securitization model.

The third major form of mortgage finance is the "mortgage or covered bond," popular in continental Europe, especially in Denmark, Germany, France, and Spain. Covered bonds are issued

by banks and share many features with MBS, but they also differ in important ways. Most importantly, investors in covered bonds have a general claim on the issuing bank; but in the event that the issuing bank defaults, the investor can claim the underlying mortgage collateral. (This structure is similar to the structure of "repo" transactions and advances from the Federal Home Loan Bank System to its members.) This structure provides two layers of protection for the covered bond investor: the bank's equity and the housing collateral.

The covered bond model has another advantage relative to the MBS model. When a Danish mortgage bank grants a mortgage, it is obliged to sell an equivalent bond with a maturity and cash flow that matches those of the underlying loan almost perfectly. When the price of that bond falls, the homeowner can purchase that bond to partially pay off her mortgage. This mechanism prevents the kind of price drops in the securitization market that the United States has experienced. As such, the covered bond markets seem to offer a liquidity benefit attributed to securitization but also to contain the moral hazard in lending (due to full recourse to the issuing bank's balance sheet).

7.1.2 Types of Mortgage Products

Table 7.1 shows the typical mortgage characteristics in different countries and the types of mortgage products that were available as of 2005. In the United States, the standard mortgage product is the 30-year fixed-rate, self-amortizing, prepayable mortgage. Nominal payments are fixed, and borrowers are protected from fluctuations in interest rates. If rates rise, payments are unchanged. If rates decline, borrowers typically have the option to refinance at no explicit cost (except for the normal transactions costs of the refinance process). The market share of fixed-rate mortgages (FRMs) fluctuates over time, but has averaged around 70% in the United States.[2] Denmark, the home of the covered bond, is the only other country where the prepayable 30-year FRM is widely popular.

In many other countries, such as the United Kingdom, Canada, and Australia (which also have reasonably well-developed securitization markets), long-term fixed rate mortgage products are not widely available. The default product is an adjustable-rate mortgage (ARM), where the interest rate is tied to the short-term government interest rate, or a "hybrid mortgage," which has a short initial period of a fixed rate followed by an extended period of variable rates. The latter are popular in Canada, Germany, and the Netherlands. Japan has fixed-term loans, where the borrower has the option to choose a new fixed rate or an adjustable rate at the end of the first fixed-rate period. Also, many countries have prepayment fees (as shown in the last column of table 7.1).

The dominant form of mortgage is closely tied to the funding mechanism. In countries with deposit-based funding, adjustable rate products are more common because they provide the banks that hold the mortgages on their balance sheets with a better match for their short-term adjustable rate deposits, exposing the banks

TABLE 7.1
Mortgages Terms across Different Countries

	Typical LTV	Maximum LTV	For 2nd mortgage	Mortgage debt to GDP	Fixed-term range 10–20 years	Fixed-term range 20+ years	Repayment by fee-free redemption
United States	75%	97%	A	69%	A	A	A
Denmark	80%	80%	A	70%	A	A	A
France	67%	100%	L	25%	A	L	N
Germany	67%	80%	A	53%	A	L	N
Italy	55%	80%	A	13%	L	L	N
Netherlands	90%	115%	A	100%	A	L	N
Portugal	83%	90%	A	51%	N	N	N
Spain	70%	100%	A	42%	L	L	N
United Kingdom	69%	110%	A	69%	L	N	L
Japan	80%	80%		36%	A	A	L
Korea	40%	75%	N	14%	L	N	A
Canada	65%	90%	A	44%	N	N	N
Australia	63%	80%	A	74%	N	N	L

Source: Richard K. Green and Susan M. Wachter, "The American Mortgage in Historical and International Context," *Journal of Economic Perspectives* 19 (4, 2005): 101.

Key: A = available; L = limited availability; N = no availability.

to less interest rate risk. In contrast, 30-year prepayable mortgages expose banks to substantial maturity mismatch and interest rate risk. These risks are hard to hedge. Hence, banks are eager to sell off such loans to the secondary market in the form of MBS, rather than holding them. This is true for the United States and Denmark, although, as mentioned in chapter 2, a considerable amount of MBS were held within the banking sector. In the United States, the government support through the GSEs was crucial to get the securitization market off the ground in the 1970s. In the United Kingdom also, where banks have begun to employ various forms of securitization to fund mortgage risks, there has been some rise in the fixed-rate and hybrid-form mortgages.

7.1.3 The Size of Mortgage Markets

Table 7.1 also indicates large differences in how much mortgage debt households are taking on, relative to the size of the economy. In Italy and Korea, mortgage debt is below 15% of GDP, whereas in the Netherlands it is 100% of GDP. Updated numbers show that Denmark's ratio had grown to 95% by 2008, comparable to the Netherlands' ratio of 99%. The United Kingdom and Ireland both had mortgage-debt-to-GDP ratios of 80%. For comparison, the U.S. mortgage-debt-to-GDP ratio at the end of 2008 was 92%, twice as high as the European Union (EU) average (27 countries) of 47%. Some of this size difference is attributable to the fact that countries such as Denmark, Germany, and Italy maintain a minimum 20% down payment requirement (or a maximum 80% loan-to-value ratio (LTV); see Table 7.1). Nevertheless, as numbers for Denmark and the Netherlands illustrate, the United States is no outlier, given its much larger government involvement.

7.1.4 The Extent of Government Support, and Home Ownership Rates

Clearly, the United States is an outlier in its government involvement in mortgage markets, providing much more support than does any other country. We discuss the various programs to support home ownership in chapter 9, and of course, there are the GSEs. While many countries have affordable housing programs for low-income households, like the Federal Housing Administration (FHA) in the United States, very few have GSE Godzillas like Freddie Mac and Fannie Mae. Two exceptions are Canada and Japan, but the market share of government-backed institutions is significantly less than that of the United States, and the securitization market is substantially smaller to begin with. In particular, since 1945, the Canada Mortgage and Housing Corporation has insured the principal and interest on around $135 billion of first residential mortgage loans, a far cry from what Fannie and Freddie have guaranteed. And in Japan, the Government Housing Loan Corporation directly lent to households, but has been replaced by the Japan Housing Finance Agency to focus on securitization instead.

Importantly, unlike the experience in the United States, the GSEs of other countries have not experienced exceptional losses or required government capital injections. The reason is that these institutions take on no significant credit and interest rate risk, as they have limited or no investment portfolios, and have no formal affordable housing policy mandate (like Fannie's and Freddie's mission goals). Ultimately, the U.S. government's being hand in glove with the GSEs, rather than at arm's length, has allowed these institutions to grow to a size and complexity where the financial markets perceive them to be guaranteed fully for all practical purposes. This has lowered the GSEs' cost of borrowing and allowed them to grow even further. Hence, in spite of experiencing similar housing price collapses to that of the United States, no other country faces the uphill task of overhauling mortgage finance and reconsidering the extent of government involvement.

Because home ownership has been such an important goal in the United States, one might argue that (at least some of) the trauma might have been worthwhile, because all of the subsidies

TABLE 7.2
An International Comparison of Home Ownership Rates

Rank	Country	Ownership Rate (%)	Date	Source
1	Singapore	89	2009	Statistics Singapore
2	Spain	85	2008	European Mortgage Federation
3	Iceland	83	2005	Statistics Iceland (HES survey)
4	Belgium	78	2007	European Mortgage Federation
5	Norway	77	2001	UN Economic Commission for Europe
6	Portugal	76	2007	European Mortgage Federation
7	Luxembourg	75	2008	European Mortgage Federation
8	Ireland	75	2009	European Mortgage Federation
9	Chile	73	2002	UN Housing Policy
10	Italy	72	2007	INSEE and Eurostat
11	Israel	71	2004	UN Economic Commission for Europe
12	Australia	70	2006	Australian Bureau of Statistics
13	England	68	2010	Building Societies Association
14	Canada	68	2006	Statistics Canada
15	Sweden	68	2008	European Mortgage Federation
16	New Zealand	68	2001	Statistics New Zealand
17	United States	67	2009	U.S. Census Bureau
18	Japan	61	2003	Japan Statistical Yearbook 2005
19	Finland	59	2008	Statistics Finland
20	Czech Republic	59	2007	European Mortgage Federation
21	France	57	2007	European Mortgage Federation
22	Netherlands	57	2008	European Mortgage Federation
23	Austria	56	2009	Statistics Austria
24	Denmark	54	2009	European Mortgage Federation
25	Germany	46	2007	INSEE and Eurostat
26	Switzerland	35	2000	Statistics Switzerland

Source: Alex J. Pollock, Testimony before the Subcommittee on Security and International Trade and Finance, Committee on Banking, Housing and Urban Affairs, U.S. Senate, September 29, 2010.

and policies might have allowed the United States to have a far superior home ownership rate, as compared to that in other developed countries. As the data in table 7.2 indicate, though, this is simply not the case. Other developed countries (Germany is the lone substantial outlier in the table) have been able to sustain comparable or even higher rates of home ownership, without the elaborate subsidies and policy apparatus that has characterized U.S. housing policy and mortgage finance policy. And to the extent that home ownership rates also are indicative of comparative house affordability, the same conclusion stands.

7.1.5 Bankruptcy Legislation Relating to Mortgage Defaults

In the United States, many states legislate that a mortgage lender has no recourse to any other assets besides the house when a borrower defaults on her mortgage.[3] In other U.S. states, there is recourse but only through a complicated and lengthy court process that banks in practice often forgo. In sharp contrast, many countries in continental Europe have unlimited recourse: not only to all of the other assets of the delinquent borrower but also to her future wages. Research has shown—and it is common wisdom—that countries with stronger recourse upon default experience fewer mortgage foreclosures. Put simply, homeowners in Belgium do not default on their mortgages because lenders will come after everything that they own plus all future wages until the debt is fully repaid. Such recourse also makes it easier to repossess the house if necessary (it is faster and less costly). For example, Denmark's legal system with "enforcement courts" makes it easier for a bank to seize the home of a defaulter, whereas the U.S. foreclosure process is deemed to be rather cumbersome (except in the "one action statute" states of California, Idaho, Montana, Nevada, New York, and Utah, where the lenders are permitted only a single lawsuit to collect mortgage debt, following which they typically must take foreclosure action).

7.2 THE BOOM-BUST CYCLE ACROSS THE GLOBE

In light of the important differences in how mortgage markets work in different countries, it is interesting to consider how they fared during the recent credit cycle. After all, the financial crisis and the Great Recession of 2008–9 were a worldwide phenomenon. Nevertheless, the United States and Europe were hit much harder than were the developing economies in Asia and Latin America—notably China, India, and Brazil. The developing economies experienced sharp stock market crashes in 2008 but rebounded dramatically in 2009. The same holds true for the decline in housing markets. There has, however, been considerable variation in the boom-bust cycle of housing credit and prices even among the developed economies. An important question is whether there is any systematic link between the institutional setup of housing finance in these countries and how well the housing and mortgage markets held up during the crisis.

Table 7.3 shows the evolution of house prices around the world. In every country, house prices are normalized to be 100 in the first quarter of 1996. The second column shows the level of house prices at the peak of the housing boom, as well as when house prices peaked. Ireland had the largest run-up, with house prices more than quadrupling by the first quarter of 2007. Britain and Spain also saw house prices more than triple. Australia and France come in just before the United States. Canada had a much more modest boom than did the United States, while Japan (and also Germany, which is not in the table) had no boom at all. In fact, house prices in both countries were falling rather than going up.

The bust hit the United States, the United Kingdom, Ireland, and Spain especially hard. House prices in Ireland and Spain are now at their lowest point since the decline started. Compared to the 34% fall from the peak in the United States, house prices fell 35% from peak in Ireland, 18% in Britain, and 13% in Spain.

Table 7.3
House Price Boom and Bust across Countries

1996.Q1 = 100	Peak	Trough	Current (2010.Q2)
Ireland	420 (2007.Q1)	275 (2010.Q2)	275
Britain	350 (2007.Q4)	290 (2009.Q1)	325
Spain	310 (2008.Q1)	275 (2010.Q2)	275
Australia	290 (2008.Q1)	275 (2009.Q1)	340
Denmark	270 (2007.Q3)	220 (2009.Q2)	225
France	255 (2008.Q1)	235 (2009.Q2)	240
United States	240 (2006.Q2)	160 (2009.Q1)	165
Canada	170 (2008.Q2)	160 (2009.Q2)	165
Japan	100 (1996.Q1)	60 (2010.Q2)	60

Source: Economist House Price Indicators, July 8, 2010 and interactive tool http://www.economist.com/blogs/freeexchange/2010/10/global_house_prices.

In sharp contrast, Canada, Australia, France, and Germany all but avoided a downturn in housing markets. While there was a housing boom globally, it is clear that the boom-bust pattern was most severe in the United States, the United Kingdom, Ireland, and Spain.

The recovery also seems to be proceeding at different speeds across the globe. In sharp contrast with the slow recovery in house prices in the United States (+4.5% in the first quarter of 2010 compared to a year earlier) or the declines in Ireland (-11.0%) and Spain (-4.7%), Singapore (+38%), Hong Kong (+28%), Australia (+20%), South Africa (+15%), and China (+12%) have all seen strong growth. Even Britain has seen increases in house prices of nearly 9% over the last year, reversing the bust. On the basis of historical price-rent ratios, this latest run-up leaves house prices at elevated levels relative to rents in several countries. The *Economist* calculates "over-valuation" as of August 2010 of 61% in Australia, 54% in Hong Kong, and 34% in Britain, causing concerns of froth in these housing markets. In response, Australia, Singapore, Hong Kong, and China have raised interest rates or have tightened borrowing requirements. In contrast, house prices-to-rent ratios in the United States are 6.5% *below* their long-term average. Japan never recovered from the real estate bubble of 1989, and its housing is now 35% cheaper than the historical average.

What are the contributing factors to this cross-country variation in the boom-bust pattern and subsequent recovery?

Mortgage credit growth was perhaps the important facilitator of fast house price appreciation during the boom. There was rapid growth in the ratio of mortgage debt to GDP between 1998 and 2008 in many countries: 53% in Ireland, 38% in Spain and in the Netherlands, 30% in the United Kingdom, but only 16% in France, 12% in Italy, and even -6% in Germany. As in the United States, houses prices rose much faster than did incomes in Spain, Ireland, the United Kingdom, New Zealand, and even France, forcing households to increase their debt levels to afford housing. With 1996 as a benchmark year (100), the ratio of house price to average income climbed to 270 in Ireland, 200 in New Zealand, 170 in Spain, 160 in Australia, 150 in Japan, and 130 in the United States. Germany is the exception, with house prices falling 20% compared to income between 2004 and 2009.

The deterioration of lending standards was another significant factor. We discuss this phenomenon in the United States in detail in chapter 3. No other country saw a comparable slide in the quality of mortgages that were issued. The main reason is that the subprime market did not develop to the same extent in other countries, because of stricter regulation of the financial sector and its better enforcement,[4] the absence of a formal government mandate to encourage affordable home ownership, and the small presence (if any) of government-sponsored enterprises in mortgage markets. This may have prevented a U.S.-style race-to-the-bottom.

In the aftermath of the crisis, many countries saw a tightening of mortgage lending standards, including countries that saw a smaller deterioration in standards during the run-up. In the United States, 65% of lenders reported tightening standards, while that number was 80% in the Netherlands. The use of 100%

LTV loans and limited-documentation loans has essentially disappeared around the globe (both the United States and the United Kingdom featured a significant increase in such loans during the credit boom). The almost complete collapse of private-sector mortgage lending and securitization (in the nonconforming segment) was also unique to the United States. And although similar to the United States, the United Kingdom saw a 30% drop in lending during and right after the crisis, while Denmark saw no drop-off in volume.

Finally, another factor has affected the speed of recovery of housing markets: whether the mortgage credit boom was a purely financial phenomenon or was also accompanied by a construction boom that led to an oversupply of homes. In the United States and Spain, there was at least in hindsight a massive misallocation of the economy's resources to construction. The oversupply is contributing to the substantial unemployment rate in Spain and the United States at present. It has even led the chief economist of Fannie Mae to call for tearing down some housing developments built during the boom. In contrast, there was not as much of a construction boom in the United Kingdom (apparently thanks to a somewhat more bureaucratic planning office). The lower inventory of housing has facilitated the house price recovery there. Hence, while house prices rocketed skyward with the easing of credit and bottomed when credit tightened, there is no shadow inventory of excess houses that would prevent the normal demand-based recovery of house prices.

7.3 "BAD BANKS": RING OUT THE OLD, RING IN THE NEW!

While not all countries have the misfortune of having created behemoths out of government-sponsored enterprises, many have their own share of misguided policies for federal- or municipal-owned banks and, in general, for the regulation of the financial sector.

One of the first banks to collapse and be bailed out in the financial crisis of 2007–9 was the German Sachsen Landesbank. The bank had provided credit guarantees of more than three times its equity capital to off-balance-sheet vehicles, which were funded by short-term debt and invested in long-term and illiquid credit assets. The bank was unable to fulfill promises under these guarantees and was rendered insolvent, not unlike Fannie and Freddie. Germany, in fact, has a large number of such regional banks (called *Landesbanken*), which are owned by state governments. Many of these were "bad banks" that were set up in previous crises to deal with poor-quality assets. Before 2005, the Landesbanken operated with guarantees by their respective state governments, which significantly lowered their funding costs. In 2001 the European Union decided that such guarantees violated EU competition law and required the state governments to abandon state guarantees by 2005. However, all debt issued before 2005 still benefited from grandfathered state guarantees until 2015.

As a result, many Landesbanken issued debt—indeed, aggressively so—before 2005 in order to avail themselves of their last chance to raise financing at lower funding costs. However, what were the Landesbanken to do with this financing? In search of a "new business model," they plunged headlong into the residential and commercial mortgages of the United States, the United Kingdom, and the rest of Europe, taking on tremendous leverage (several times that of Fannie and Freddie). They collapsed in August 2007, on the first day that the markets worried about the quality of assets and guarantees backing the special-purpose vehicles.

On the one hand, the fate of German Landesbanken illustrates the reach of global capital markets. The U.S. and the U.K. housing booms were fueled—and put at risk—not just by their domestic financial sectors but also by foreign ones. On the other hand, it illustrates the risk of government institutions' veering away from their original mission and placing vast amounts of taxpayer money at risk because of the combination of subsidies and guarantees.

The conditions at the Spanish *Cajas*—savings banks that were originally aimed at creating the habit of thrift among the very poor but that evolved out of this charitable objective to become private commercial banks—has not been much different. The Cajas fueled the credit and construction boom in Spain, with their lending standards' highlighting the poor governance of government-owned financial institutions and the collective risk from them even when each is individually small. In fact, because of competition from local Cajas, the large global Spanish banks struggled somewhat unsuccessfully to get their hands into the housing pie—something that turned out to be a boon in disguise. Large Spanish banks such as Santander entered the crisis with robust balance sheets and have in fact been the purchasers of last resort in the financial sectors of other countries.

These failed government enterprises—Fannie and Freddie, the Landesbanken, the Cajas, and the like, all of which were set up with an initial government mission, followed by a "mission creep" and eventually by the mission's going awry—are now being addressed or overhauled (or, at least, are being brought under greater scrutiny). The emerging risk, however, is that the resolution of other failed private institutions with massive government recapitalization or outright nationalization is creating a new vintage of government-owned financial firms.

In the United Kingdom Northern Rock, one of the top five mortgage lenders, was heavily exposed to U.S. subprime mortgages. Not being able to roll over its short-term funding, it received a liquidity lifeline from the Bank of England in September 2007 and promptly suffered the first bank run in the United Kingdom in 150 years. It collapsed and was nationalized in February 2008. In January 2010 the bank was split into a "bad bank," which contains the assets, and a "good bank," which continues the banking activities. The U.K. Treasury also infused £37 billion ($64 billion) of new capital into the Royal Bank of Scotland Group plc, Lloyds TSB, and HBOS plc, to avert a financial-sector collapse in October 2008. The government provided more loan guarantees to the banking system in January 2009 in an effort to restart personal and business lending. After experiencing massive losses, the government's stake in RBS was raised to 84% in November 2009. The question of when the government will exit these stakes is constantly under debate.

Similar emergency recapitalizations occurred throughout Europe (Fortis in Belgium, Luxembourg, and the Netherlands; Commerzbank in Germany; and Anglo Irish Bank and the Bank of Ireland in Ireland). For instance, with its banking sector particularly exposed to real estate debt and suffering from collapsing real estate prices, Ireland was the first EU country to create a "bad bank": the National Asset Management Agency (NAMA) in November 2009. It bought €77 billion in toxic real estate loans from Irish banks at about a 50% discount. These loans were purchased by issuing additional government debt, explicitly accounting for the cost on the budget. The low prices, compared to the book values of these assets, caused new capital shortfalls in the summer of 2010.

And the saga continues. Many large banks of Western European countries are either explicitly owned by the government, are being run as "bad banks" of this crisis, or are living only because of oxygen provided by asset or debt guarantees from the government. Will these institutions in due course sow the seeds of the next financial crisis? More likely than not. For now, the proportion of finance that is controlled by Western European governments—just like the GSEs in the United States—is only rising. Even if global economic growth rebounds to propel us out of the economic malaise, this footprint of the government interventions may come to haunt us, and every effort should be made to erase it in good times.

8

HOW TO REFORM A BROKEN SYSTEM

> As the housing and mortgage markets recover, the Fed's support for the GSEs will end, and private capital will return. Fannie and Freddie should not then be allowed to revert to their old form, crowding out private competition and putting taxpayers on the hook for failure while shareholders benefit from success. . . . At a minimum, the GSEs should be restructured to eliminate the systemic risk they posed. An easy way to address this is to shrink them by reducing their investment portfolios—and their huge debt loads. I also believe that their mission should be curtailed significantly to reduce the subsidy for *homeownership* that helped create the crisis. It is important to leave room for a robust private-sector secondary mortgage market that serves the taxpayers and homeowners equally well.
>
> —*Henry M Paulson Jr., ex-Treasury Secretary, in* On the Brink, *2010*

While chapters 5 and 6 provided the pros and cons of having the GSEs as a policy tool in the midst of a crisis, this chapter focuses on how we envision fixing the GSEs in the long run. It is clearly a formidable task; but, as the various quotes in this book have reminded us, many minds have thought about the problem for more than a decade—in relatively quiet times and also in turbulent ones—and arrived at common solutions. They seem to suggest a retrenchment of the government role in mortgage finance in order to enable private markets in securitization to grow and flourish. Yet, we run the real risk that the current condition of the housing markets might in the end lead to a government decision that does not resist the temptation of using the GSEs for one more function: propping up the housing market in a crisis rather than contributing to one.

We outlined the many roles that the GSEs have played: as a tool for promoting home ownership, as a tool to fight income inequality and foreclosures, and even as a monetary policy tool. By combining all of these functions, the GSEs were unfit to conduct any one of their functions well. And they became gigantic and complex institutions that were too big to fail. The securities that they issued or backed represented the largest fixed-income market in the world at the time (now the Treasury market is larger). Any substantial loss of value would do considerable harm to their largest holders: the financial sector and other countries. This reality adds further pressure to the federal government to continue to prop up the housing market. We argue that this is an unsustainable and undesirable state of affairs. A viable long-term solution must radically overhaul the housing finance system in the United States and build it back from the ground up.

The goal of reforming the housing finance is to ensure an efficient mortgage market, both in primary (origination) and in secondary mortgage markets. If the origination quality of the mortgages in MBS pools is poor, secondary markets can suffer from severe information problems. Conversely, if secondary markets are illiquid or systematically underprice risk, they provide incentives to mortgage lenders to originate poor-quality loans. Hence, by an "efficient" mortgage market, we have in mind a housing finance system with the following characteristics:

1. Such a system does not engender moral hazard issues in mortgage origination and securitization.
2. If any market failures exist, a housing finance system corrects them; notable in this case is the externality from undertaking too much credit and interest rate risk, as this risk is inherently systemic in nature.
3. It maintains a level playing field between the different financial players in the mortgage market to limit a concentrated build-up of systemic risk.
4. The system features market pricing of risks as well as charging for implicit or explicit government guarantees.

According to chapters 1–5 of this book, there should be little doubt that the current mortgage finance system falls far short of these goals. In particular, moral hazard is rampant as financial institutions—the GSEs, other large and complex financial firms, and FDIC depository institutions—load up on mortgage risk knowing that they are insulated from its full consequences. Indeed, economists Nadezhda Malysheva and John Walter at the Federal Reserve Bank of Richmond find that 59% of all liabilities of the financial sector now come under a safety net.[1] Because this safety net either is not priced or is underpriced, large distortions occur, such as subsidized financing of financial firms and the loss of market discipline. Somewhat perversely, the problem is all the more worsened by the financial firms' becoming systemically important and thus too big to fail: the implicit government guarantee gets more ingrained, and the negative impact is that much more. And rather than the regulatory system's discouraging this behavior, it is actually encouraged. The combination of GSEs and commercial banks or thrifts in a securitized mortgage finance system has less than 30% of the capital requirements of traditional banking. No wonder we are where we are.

It should be clear then that mortgage markets operate in the broader context of the financial system and its existing infrastructure and regulation. The Dodd-Frank Act of 2010 is likely to affect this broader context in nontrivial ways by regulating origination, securitization, and rating aspects of mortgage finance. Given the undesirable state of mortgage finance in the United States at the present moment, transition issues must be addressed on the road toward the desired long-term reform.

How much—and in what form—should government involvement persist in the long-term reform of mortgage finance? As a fundamental principle, government involvement should be present only to the extent that it improves the efficiency of the reformed housing finance system, as outlined previously. This is the best way to minimize costs to taxpayers, in sharp contrast with the seemingly endless losses that we witnessed with Fannie and Freddie. Such an efficient system can restore liquidity in the moribund markets for mortgage-backed securities (MBS), facilitate efficient risk sharing across different institutions and households, and support a wider availability of fairly priced mortgages.

Recall that the GSEs currently perform two functions: *portfolio or investment function*, in which they buy and retain mortgages and mortgage-backed securities; and *guarantee function*, in which they underwrite the credit risk of mortgages to facilitate the pass-through of their interest and principal payments to capital market participants and financial firms. Also, the GSEs operate in two markets: conforming mortgages (subject to size limits, low LTVs, high credit scores, good income coverage ratios, etc.); and nonconforming mortgages (the rest). As we will explain, these two functions and the two markets require slightly different reforms to ensure that our efficiency criteria are met.

Our preferred reform proposal involves the following steps. First, the investment function of the GSEs needs to be discontinued entirely. Second, we discuss how to structure the guarantee function of the GSEs. It should be reworked to better balance systemic risk, efficient pricing, and market discipline. One of the conclusions is that public guarantees should be restricted to conforming mortgages. Therefore, the final set of recommendations discusses how to deal with nonconforming mortgages and, in particular, where these mortgages fit into the broader regulatory structure of the Dodd-Frank Wall Street Reform and Consumer Protection Act of 2010. In chapter 9, we discuss the economics of subsidizing home ownership. We recommend that the government's affordable home ownership objectives be substantially shrunk in size, remain prefunded at all times, and be housed in the Federal Housing Administration (FHA) and/or elsewhere in the Department of Housing and Urban Development (HUD) instead of being entangled with the objective of developing a healthy secondary market for mortgage securitization.

8.1 DISCONTINUE THE INVESTMENT FUNCTION OF THE GSES

As we discussed in detail in chapter 1, the GSEs not only guarantee conforming mortgages held by other investors but also actively invest in a large portfolio of mortgage assets—the so-called retained portfolio. At the end of 2009, Freddie and Fannie either guaranteed or owned $5.39 trillion dollars in mortgages, fully $1.71 trillion of which (27% of the total) was owned in portfolio. This 27% retained mortgage share is down from 44% in 2002 but is only slightly below the 2008 all-time dollar high of $1.76 trillion.

The rationale for this retained portfolio was to promote liquidity in the secondary mortgage market. Higher liquidity, it was believed, could make secondary mortgage markets more efficient and would ultimately trickle down to homeowners in the form of lower mortgage rates. We believe that this reasoning is obsolete at best and probably false. It is obsolete because the market for conforming mortgage-backed securities is one of the largest and most liquid fixed-income markets in the world. By now, markets have had almost 40 years of experience in trading conforming mortgage-backed securities. We believe that they do not need continued liquidity support in the form of proprietary trading purchases from the GSEs. It is potentially false, because there is no evidence for a direct link between the size of the GSE portfolios and the liquidity of secondary mortgage markets.[2]

In reality, the retained portfolio management business became the cash cow of the GSEs. Rather than making markets more liquid, it had as its true objective to make money for the shareholders, traders, and CEOs of the GSEs, just as is true of any other hedge fund. The CEOs gained enormously: Richard Syron of Freddie Mac and Daniel Mudd of Fannie Mae each took home $28 million in 2006 and 2007 alone. Ominously, these were exactly the years that the GSEs ramped up the risk of their portfolios the most. Even under the current conservatorship, compensation seems excessive. For 2010, the Treasury Department and the Federal Housing Finance Agency approved CEO compensation of $6 million each, including $2 million incentive payments for each executive. In sharp contrast, Benjamin Bernanke, the chairman of the Federal Reserve earns $191,000 per year, or 30 times less.

The nature of the retained portfolio business invites comparison with the hedge fund industry. To put the GSEs' $1.7 trillion retained portfolio into perspective, the total assets under management of the entire hedge fund industry were $2 trillion at the end of 2009. Given aggregate leverage ratios around 5, this means that hedge function industry has a balance sheet on the order of $10 trillion. The largest hedge fund in 2009 was Bridgewater Associates with $38 billion. Freddie and Fannie's trading operation therefore was around 20% as large as the entire hedge fund industry, and the two GSEs were magnitudes bigger than the largest hedge fund.

The level of sophistication of the GSEs' trading function rivaled that of premier hedge funds. They employed sophisticated quantitative models for predicting the performance of mortgage loans, and they used large derivative positions to manage interest rate and default risk. This trading function generated enormous revenues: about $28 billion in each of 2002, 2003, and 2004. After a dip, the trading revenue was $31 billion in 2009. In fact, throughout its history net interest income (from such investment activities) has surpassed guarantee fee income (from the traditional guarantee business). Over the past 15 years, trading revenues represented on average 73% of all revenues.

Like many hedge funds, the GSEs increased the riskiness of their mortgage portfolios in the years leading up to the crisis. They purchased $227 billion worth of subprime and Alt-A mortgage-backed securities in 2006 and 2007, in addition to possibly $500 billion more of high-risk mortgages that were not classified as such.

Until the crisis of 2007–9, the GSEs appeared to be highly profitable compared to almost any other financial institution, including most hedge funds, as witnessed by their return on equity (even though they were losing the race to the bottom, which we outlined in chapter 3). Freddie's ROE averaged 23% per year from 1977 to 2006 and Fannie's averaged 17%. In the last 10 years of this period, Fannie's ROE was 23%. Part of this stellar performance is attributable to their ability to borrow at below-market rates because of their implicit government backing (see chapter 1), and part is due to the GSEs' taking on tail risk, earning consistent spreads in normal times albeit at the risk of significant losses during an economic downturn.

Our first long-term policy recommendation is to *discontinue the trading function of the GSEs*. We believe that there is no role for a gigantic government-sponsored hedge fund that trades in mortgage-related contracts. The trading function in many respects highlights the worst aspects of a "privatize the gains, socialize the losses" entity. By being able to borrow cheaply, the GSEs invested in a highly levered portfolio of increasingly risky mortgages to boost profits. When the credit risk that they took on materialized, the taxpayer was stuck with a huge bill, a significant proportion of which represents the losses of the retained mortgage portfolios.

8.1.1 Transition

What to do with the $1.7 trillion portfolio of assets? We envision that the government could slowly wind down the assets on the GSEs' balance sheets—for example, by corralling them into a "GSE Resolution Trust Corporation" (GSE RTC). A similar structure was established during the savings and loan (S&L) crisis in the late 1980s and early 1990s in the United States and during banking crises in other countries (e.g., Sweden in the early 1990s).

Specifically, the Resolution Trust Corporation (RTC) was set up after the S&L crisis in 1989 with the intention of being a "bad bank" (technically a U.S. government-owned asset management company). It took over the loss-ridden assets (which included commercial properties, commercial mortgages, and residential mortgages) of troubled S&Ls and was charged with the business of liquidating these assets. In six years, the RTC closed or otherwise resolved 747 thrifts with total assets of $394 billion. In 1995 its duties were transferred to the reformed and empowered Federal Deposit Insurance Corporation (FDIC). The RTC pioneered the use of "equity partnerships" to help liquidate the real estate and financial assets that it inherited from insolvent thrift institutions. While different structures were used, all of the equity partnerships involved a private-sector partner's acquiring a partial interest in a pool of assets, controlling the management and sale of the assets in the pool, and making distributions to the RTC reflective of the RTC's retained interest. Although the prices that the RTC received on its initial "bulk sales" were often considered disappointing, the RTC did much better in the partnerships. It kept some of the upside through a retained interest and through the partnerships benefited from expertise of private liquidators and asset administrators that it would have otherwise struggled to put together or acquire.

All in all, the RTC represents exactly the kind of bad bank that should be set up at the end of a crisis. It was a boring public utility in the sense that its only task was to liquidate real-estate-related assets; its clarity of function and focus facilitated innovative methods that did not simply retain the risk of bad assets it took on but, in fact, involved the private sector in facilitating liquidations; and it eventually died (was wound down and dissolved), leaving no footprints of a government entity into the indefinite future. We envision the GSE RTC formalizing the current role of the GSEs as a "bad bank."

The main task of the GSE RTC would be to wind down the $1.7 trillion dollar mortgage portfolio. Given the size of the portfolio, the approach will have to be gradual lest it destabilize MBS prices (the fire-sale argument of chapter 4) and ultimately mortgage rates in the primary mortgage market.

The first step would be a reduction in *new loan purchases*. Given the fragile state of the housing market, a cold-turkey approach that immediately stops any new purchases seems imprudent. Thus, GSE reform should start with the firm intention to reduce new GSE purchases for investment purposes to zero over the first three to five years of the transition.

The second step is to reduce the existing assets in the retained portfolio. Part of the reduction in portfolio will occur automatically as mortgage loans mature, default, or are prepaid. This could occur rather quickly. The average annual pay-down rate of the GSEs' portfolios from 1997 to 2004 was about 25%. In addition, we recommend that the GSEs draw firm plans actively to sell assets in portfolio to a variety of private market participants, such as hedge funds, pension funds, sovereign wealth funds, or other institutional investors.

As part of the conservatorship agreement, the Treasury has put forth a plan along these lines. The original conservatorship agreement stipulated that each of the GSEs should reduce its retained portfolio to $850 billion by December 31, 2009. Afterward, it envisioned a 10% annual reduction each year until each portfolio was reduced to $250 billion. In May 2009, the limit for 2009 was raised to $900 billion, probably in anticipation of an early breach of the original agreement. Indeed, at the end of

2009, Fannie's retained portfolio was $869 billion (down only $43 billion from 2008), while Freddie's was $840 billion (down $9 billion). The new rules imply a December 31, 2010, limit on the portfolio of each GSE of $810 billion. The 10% reduction in this asset limit will lead to a 2011 limit of $729 billion, a 2012 limit of $656 billion, and so forth. Under this schedule, the portfolio will fall below $250 billion in 2021.

We believe that the gradual winding down of the portfolio is a good plan. By putting a cap on the overall size of the portfolio, it allows for some new purchases to the extent that the existing portfolio shrinks fast enough. By announcing an average annual percentage reduction in the portfolio, the private market can form expectations about future conditions in the mortgage market and plan accordingly. However, the swift modification of the agreement in 2009, less than a year after the agreement had been in place, does not bode well for the future. It highlights the potential for future backsliding at the discretion of the politicians in charge. We recommend that a firm plan be included in a GSE reform bill, with strict enforcement, and that the plan be kept in place until the *entire portfolio* is sold off. The FHFA should be given authority to exercise strict oversight over this process.

Finally, we recommend that the reduction of the portfolio should be accelerated beyond the 10% annual reduction whenever market conditions allow. As housing market conditions improve and foreclosures return to normal levels, the prices for mortgage-backed securities (MBS) will stabilize and improve as well. When this happens, the GSE RTC should accelerate its sales to private-market participants. While the cost of an accelerated exit may be to affect prices adversely, the benefit is to minimize the risk to the taxpayer that stems from declines in the value of the mortgage portfolio when interest rates increase from their historically low levels. The only goal of the GSE RTC would be to wind down the portfolio in a fashion that minimizes the present value of losses to taxpayers.

The preceding analysis also suggests a way for the Federal Reserve to act in a similar manner. As we explained in chapter 6, the Federal Reserve now owns $1.25 trillion in GSE MBS and $175 billion of agency debt. As with the retained mortgage portfolio, an accelerated sale of these holdings would prevent future losses due to rising mortgage rates, but doing it in an unfavorable environment would further depress MBS prices. To avoid depressing MBS prices too much, a measured pace of divestment seems to be the best course of action.

An additional argument for a faster rather than a slower divestment is that monetary policy should not be influenced by the Fed's holdings of MBS. It is easy to imagine a scenario where interest rates are kept too low for too long in order to avoid losses on the MBS portfolio held by the GSEs or by the Fed itself. Such considerations fly in the face of sound monetary policy, which should focus on overall price stability in the economy. This last consideration makes the Federal Reserve a less-than-ideal candidate to be the lender of last resort in U.S. housing markets. In chapter 6 we proposed a new mortgage liquidity facility at the Treasury Department instead. We also proposed that the Fed would pass on its purchases to such a facility shortly after purchase instead of warehousing mortgage assets. Because the facility would be prefunded with an asset limit, once that limit is reached, the bailout would end.

8.2 THE GUARANTEE FUNCTION OF THE GSES

The second main function of the GSEs, and arguably the most important one, is to guarantee the credit risk in the mortgage loans that are bundled and sold off as mortgage-backed securities to the public. While the GSEs do not own these mortgage loans, they are responsible for all losses that are due to mortgage borrowers' defaults. Our second main recommendation is that the current guarantee function of the GSEs should be revisited, with the goal of better balancing systemic risk, efficient pricing, and market discipline. The government has not announced any formal plans for the future of the guarantee function of the GSEs.

Before any discussion of various proposals, we need to address whether mortgage guarantees—private or public—are really needed for secondary mortgage markets to function. There are other credit markets, most notably the corporate bond market, that function without such guarantees. What is special about mortgages?

There are several features that are somewhat distinctive to mortgages. First, while mortgages certainly contain a number of standardized characteristics (such as loan-to-value, income-to-payment, FICO credit score), mortgages and therefore pools of mortgages (as found in MBS) are nevertheless fairly opaque and heterogeneous by nature—more so than corporate debt. Second, while some parts of the corporate debt market could falter, there is usually an alternative source of financing for corporations, such as commercial paper, bank loans, preferred stock, common stock, convertible bonds, and plain vanilla public debt issuance. There is no plan B for the mortgage market. Third, mortgage finance is at the center of economic household activity; without access to mortgage finance in difficult times, the economy would go into a tailspin.

Because mortgages are opaque, uncertainty about the credit risk of these underlying mortgages makes MBS less liquid than otherwise similar debt securities. Liquidity is the ability to convert securities immediately into cash and becomes particularly valuable to investors in times of distress. As not only the current crisis but even preceding ones, such as the collapse of Long Term Capital Management, showed, the market for MBS without credible guarantees—even safe, so-called AAA-rated MBS—can freeze temporarily or even collapse altogether, as the risk of financial firms rises, the investors' risk appetite wanes, and the demand for cash soars. Investors demand a premium for bearing such illiquidity, and that translates to higher interest rate spreads. To the extent that guarantees enhance liquidity of the secondary mortgage market, the cost of financing mortgages will be lower.

There is another reason why mortgage guarantees may be necessary at least in the short to medium term. Capital markets are not built overnight. It takes years to develop the expertise and investor base. From the investors' side, one potential advantage of keeping all conforming mortgage-backed securities guaranteed (credit-risk-free) is that an investment community with substantial human capital was built up around buying and selling default-free mortgage-backed securities. Of course, this does not mean that a similarly well-developed capital market and collection of investors cannot take root in the credit-based MBS market. However, if the past is a guide, then the experience of the recent crisis is that the investor base was not committed to the private-label credit-based MBS market.

A case in point: after the MBS market developed in the 1980s, in order to further expand the market to investors, the collateralized mortgage obligations (CMOs) market was created. CMOs took GSE MBS and broke them into prioritized tranches of prepayment and interest rate risk. The CMO market expanded rapidly from nonexistent in 1983 to less than $100 billion in 1989 to more than $300 billion in 1993. With the rapid fall in interest rates in 1993, huge losses were distributed in CMOs across capital markets, causing the CMO market to literally disappear overnight. Similar to the current crisis, the CMO collapse can be attributed to a large shock to the market—in this case, prepayments on mortgages; and too much complexity, with some CMOs' having 100 tranches or more. The happy ending, however, was that the CMO market gradually recovered, reaching issuance of $300 billion some five years later, and, five years after that in 2003, coming close to $1 trillion.

The important lesson is that it takes time for financial innovation to reach its full potential. The necessary requirement is that an investment community, through experience and expertise, needs to understand the market. No one should think that an appropriately designed MBS market that is focused on mortgage credit risk is not viable.

However, even if guarantees are correctly priced on an actuarial basis, these guarantees still come at a cost. While the moral hazard problem is mitigated once guarantees are priced, it does not disappear. This is because the actions of the mortgage lender are not fully observable, so once the premiums for the guarantees of conforming mortgages are set, the lender will be tempted to originate riskier mortgages. And the government's experience with FDIC's deposit insurance also indicates moral hazard problems in spite of charging banks with insurance premiums.[3] It is very difficult for the insurer to not be one step behind the insured.

An additional concern is that government guarantees might have less to do with creating liquid, efficient capital markets, but more with regulatory arbitrage by financial institutions that exploit the favorable capital requirements that are associated with mortgage guarantees. A reasonable question to ask is, If the purpose of the securitization of mortgages was to take advantage of the growth and efficiency of capital markets, why were so many of the MBS held within the banking sector? Chapter 1 described how the financial system—GSEs and banks together—exploited loopholes in capital regulation essentially to rearrange the deck chairs on the Titanic. Whatever structure is established going forward, it is essential that different approaches to financing identical mortgages be treated equally in terms of capital requirements. This crisis has taught us that the same way that water flows downhill, mortgage assets flow to whoever can leverage them the highest.

In the rest of this chapter, we take the pragmatic stand that at least some mortgage guarantees must be taken as given and discuss three potential routes toward reform of the guarantee business: nationalization, privatization, and a hybrid model of public and private capital.

No matter which route is chosen, we believe that it is important that the concept of a conforming mortgage be tightened again. At the heart of the problem of the current crisis, and especially the GSEs, were sliding underwriting standards. As we described in earlier chapters, the GSEs were stretching the notion of a conforming mortgage during the housing boom. For example, they often bought mortgages with loan-to-value rations that exceeded 90%. We envision that conforming loans' LTVs should never exceed 80%. We also recommend that homeowners be allowed to tap into their home equity only as long as the CLTV (first and second mortgage, and home equity loan/line of credit) does not exceed 80%. In such a scenario, the borrower always bears the first 20% of the risk of house price declines. Finally, we recommend that full documentation (e.g., income verification) be the norm for lending.

8.2.1 Nationalization

One option is to fully nationalize the guarantee business for conforming loans. Because the government owns 79.5% of the GSEs through conservatorship and because virtually all mortgages originated in 2009 and 2010 were conforming mortgages, this option is a formalization of the current situation.

Under this plan, the GSEs would effectively become a government-run *utility company*, strictly regulated, and with a fixed dollar budget. Because their budget would be on the government's books, this would end the current regime of the GSEs as off-balance-sheet special purpose vehicles of the U.S. government. CEO pay would be comparable to that of other high-ranking government servants, such as the chairman of the Federal Reserve or the Secretary of the Treasury, or perhaps the head of Ginnie Mae.

The rationale for such nationalization is that in the next large mortgage crisis, the government would inevitably bail out any private securitization firm—say, the reprivatized Freddie Mac or Fannie Mae. The advantage of the nationalization approach is that the taxpayer would not only bear the costs of the next housing market downturn and foreclosure wave but also earn the profits (the guarantee fees) in good times. In contrast to the pre-2008 situation, the government would at least earn the insurance premium for the insurance that it provides for the next earthquake in the U.S. housing market. The other advantage of this approach is that there would be no disruption in the provision of mortgage credit—not during the initial transition or in the next housing downturn.

However, there are several downsides of this approach. First, and foremost, no market information is available to ensure that the government receives the correct guarantee fee and that the guarantee function remains economically viable. The current guarantee fee of about 0.22% is clearly too low and needs to be recalibrated in case this option is employed. The history of governments' charging fees on this scale is not good. Consider deposit insurance, the other major government guarantee program. Leading up to the S&L crisis in the 1980s and the financial crisis of 2007–9, there is general agreement that deposit institutions were subsidized by below-market FDIC deposit insurance, creating moral hazard. In fact, because the FDIC's reserve fund was viewed as well capitalized, many FDIC-insured institutions were not charged at all from 1995 to 2005. Moreover, as a result of the bait-and-switch issue described previously, moral hazard likely remains even if the fee pricing problem were solved.

Second, the other major disadvantage of nationalization approach is that the government would be stuck with a huge on-balance-sheet liability at a time of large fiscal deficits and ballooning debt. Most economists would argue that the government has no comparative advantage in providing mortgage credit to most U.S. households and that it currently crowds out the private provision of mortgage credit. The preceding discussion suggests that there may be some value to allowing a credit-risky (non-guaranteed) MBS market to develop and compete openly with a guaranteed MBS market. Nationalization pretty much rules out this possibility.

Finally, government institutions tend to be poorly governed and subject to political capture. Like the GSEs, they have a tendency to morph and to be reoriented away from their intended mission toward new political goals over the course of their life. They are easy to create, but hard to manage and to abolish.

For all of these reasons, we do not favor the nationalization option.

8.2.2 Privatization

The second option is to fully privatize the guarantee business. In this scenario, the GSEs would be completely dismantled. Existing banks and mortgage lenders, as well as new lenders, would step into the breach and conduct all conforming (core) mortgage originations.

What facilitates the privatization solution is that conforming mortgages are loans that are conservatively underwritten: for example, all the loans in a pool would have loan-to-value ratios of 80% or less and have documented mortgage-payment-to-income ratios of 35% or less. Therefore, these loans would have low credit risk to begin with. Strengthening the criteria for what constitutes a conforming (core) mortgage loan would be important.

The techniques of *structured finance* could be applied to reallocate further the credit risk: the idea is to structure these loans into "tranches." The most senior tranche would effectively have no credit risk, and therefore would not need any credit guarantees. This tranche could be as large as 80% of a pool that is composed of only conforming loans: the default rate on the pool would need to exceed 40% with only a 50% recovery rate before the senior tranche would take its first dollar loss. Even in the current bust with the worst housing market for at least seven decades, the default rate on conforming mortgages has stayed well below 10%, and recovery rates are around 60%. Under this scenario, the remaining 20% of the value in a pool would be securitized as higher risk (subordinated) tranche(s) that would explicitly contain credit risk and would trade as such in private markets. To further facilitate the liquidity of these subordinated tranches, private insurance companies—such as monolines—could sell default insurance.

The rationalization for the privatization approach is that the banking sector is quite capable of doing mortgage lending to households, just as it is for providing lending to corporations and credit card lending to households. It is quite capable of pricing risky corporate loans and junk bonds, so why would it not be able to price and trade risky mortgage bonds (the junior tranches of the MBS)? The private market may currently well be crowded out of the mortgage lending market by the extensive activity of the GSEs.

The advantage of this approach is that it would eliminate the distortions that arise because of government guarantees, such as artificially low financing costs enjoyed by GSEs (or their nationalized equivalents) and the resulting low mortgage rates.

The pure privatization option, however, has several risks that would have to be managed carefully by the government or the mortgage market regulator. First, the government would have to make explicit that there will be no future bailouts of the new private mortgage players. The bankruptcy-receivership resolution mechanism for financial firms would also have to be applied to private mortgage securitizers. To make this credible, the regulator that oversees the secondary mortgage market should promote and enforce competition. The conforming mortgage lending business should become a competitive industry so that new too-big-to-fail institutions can be avoided.

The problem, however, is that a fully privatized mortgage market does not exist in a vacuum. Financial firms do not operate in a free market. The banking system is heavily regulated with government guarantees for deposit institutions; large financial institutions issue systemically risky liabilities; contrary to the goals of the new Dodd-Frank Act, too-big-to-fail has not gone away; insurance companies receive state insurance guarantees; and so on. Furthermore, mortgage origination is heavily concentrated in the four largest banks today. It is highly likely that a privatized mortgage banking system would just morph into a group of privately run "GSEs" with effective government backing. In fact, section 3.3's "Race to the Bottom" scenario laid out how this occurred in the current crisis. Given the currently vague plans of the Dodd-Frank Act to contain systemic risk resulting from the winding down of large financial firms, it is not clear that a race to the bottom would not happen again.[4]

Second, with respect to slicing and dicing the credit risks of MBS into tranches, there is a certain "déjà vu" feel to it. As the current crisis demonstrated, it is not just the credit risk of these securities that is relevant, but also their liquidity risk and model misspecification risk. If these securities cannot be converted to cash during a crisis, then the viability of tranching as a candidate to be the secondary market for mortgages needs to be questioned. As we have argued, although it may be viable over the long term, it most likely is not in the immediate future. Another issue is that the market for structured mortgage finance will have to develop more transparency and standardization to regain the confidence of its investors, but this is likely a problem that can be solved.

And then the elephant in the room—the credit rating agencies—will have to be dealt with in some way for structured mortgage finance to be credible. In the typical view of the role of ratings in the financial crisis, MBS investors were asleep at the wheel because of the government's "seal of approval" of rating agencies. But ratings were used by financial institutions to exploit capital requirements in order to hold risky MBS with little or no capital, so it was not investors who got duped here but taxpayers. This is how it worked. Because the issuer pays the agency that rates the issuer's bonds, there is a huge conflict of interest to shop the MBS tranches around until the issuer gets the desired rating, leading to inflated ratings. Because the government sets its regulatory structure around these ratings, investors such as AIG, Citigroup, ABN Amro, UBS, Merrill Lynch, Lehman, and, yes, Fannie Mae and Freddie Mac, among others, got to engage in risky activities without having to hold nearly enough of a capital buffer because of the inflated ratings. Rating agencies acquiesced in this "unholy" alliance between investors and issuers. And the taxpayers ultimately picked up the bill. While the Dodd-Frank Act makes significant headway on this issue, it is too early to determine whether the act will successfully resolve the rating agency problem.

Finally, private mortgage insurance (sold to guarantee some of the 20% junior tranches) would need to be much better capitalized than in the past. The regulation of these insurance companies should be strengthened and better enforced. There is even the issue of whether the insurance industry is equipped to offer insurance against such aggregate mortgage risk at all. It is strange to offer insurance on events that, if they occur, the insurance company cannot hope to payout.

To better understand this argument, note that, traditionally, insurers pool and diversify idiosyncratic risks with potentially catastrophic consequences for individuals and businesses. In competitive markets, insurers price diversifiable risks on an actuarial basis, yielding tremendous utility gains to the previously exposed individuals and businesses. Mortgage insurance, however, protects against macroeconomic events such as a national house price decline or a rise in unemployment and other nondiversifiable risks such as a financial market meltdown. It is not a diversifiable risk and hence carries an extra charge—"risk premium"—over and above the actuarially fair price. At the same time, mortgage insurance is far more systemically risky than are insurers' traditional activities. This sets the stage for perverse incentives for the insurance provider: sell a large amount of insurance to pocket the premium, but do not leave enough reserves (or capital) behind to honor the insurance payments. Because the payments will be due in a systemic crisis and the insurer is large, it is more likely than not that the insurer will be bailed out. At any rate, even if the insurer were not to be bailed out, it is hard to imagine that reserves will be adequately set aside for a systemic crisis, as at least some costs of the insurer's default are borne by the rest of the system.

The tale of the financial crisis of 2007–9 is that insurers provided excessive insurance on structured mortgage products that were tied to macroeconomic variables and were undercapitalized and insufficiently liquid, given the correlated risks of that insurance. For example, according to *Inside Mortgage Finance*, of the $960 billion of private mortgage insurance that was outstanding in 2007, 80% was held by just six companies: Mortgage Guaranty Insurance (21.8%), PMI Mortgage Insurance (18.8%), Radian Guaranty (14.9%), Genworth Financial (12.9%), United Guaranty (13.1%), and Republic Mortgage Insurance (11.5%). A substantial portion—$173 billion—was issued by these six insurers to satisfy the guidelines of Fannie Mae and Freddie Mac. In terms of the relative size of private and government markets, in 2007 $357 billion was newly underwritten by private insurers and $105 billion by the government insurers FHA and VA. And from January 1, 2007, to December 31, 2007, these six insurers (which were publicly traded independent companies) lost an average 60% of their stock market capitalization. Almost all of them experienced financial distress the following year. Short of banning private mortgage insurance, or requiring heavy capitalization, it is not clear how the private market can solve the systemic-risk problem. Reducing the size of the insuring firms will not work because all of the firms will fail at the same time, given the macroeconomic nature of mortgage insurance risk.

For all of these reasons, we are agnostic with respect to the complete privatization option, at least in the near future. However, if privatization was the chosen route, then the credit-risky MBS market would have to be given time to develop, and private mortgage guarantee functions may have to be fully capitalized.

During the transition to privatization, the guarantees on the existing conforming mortgages would remain in place and be assumed by the GSE RTC. In addition, new conforming mortgages could be originated by the GSE RTC, but their numbers should be reduced gradually. The wind-down scenario for the guarantee function could be set up in a similar fashion as that for the retained portfolio. In particular, new guarantees could fall at 10% per year from their 2009 peak, unless market conditions permit a faster winding down.

8.2.3 A Hybrid Solution

The question is how to balance the benefits of nationalization—the public guarantees of mortgages with its enhanced liquidity for the mortgage market—against the difficulty in pricing these guarantees and the resulting lack of market discipline, which induces moral hazard and excess risk taking. With privatization, the exact opposite is true.

While this problem appears to be intractable, there is a viable private option, in which the GSEs disappear, but all conforming mortgage-backed securities would still be guaranteed. The idea would be to form a public-private partnership for the guarantee business.

Under this scenario, private mortgage securitizers would purchase mortgage loans from originators and issue nearly default-free mortgage-backed securities. Instead of bearing the credit risk entirely themselves, private securitizers would purchase mortgage default insurance for the mortgage-backed securities. As in the previous approach, depending on the tranche structure of the MBS, mortgage insurance would be necessary for only a portion. But because this insurance still requires too much private capital to insure the—inherently systemic—credit risk of all conforming mortgages in MBS, there may be an important role for the government here. Mortgage default insurance would be offered through a new *private-public partnership* structure.

The idea behind the structure is that the private sector provides insurance with the purpose of establishing a market price for the insurance. Because the amount of private capital available to provide such systemic insurance is likely to be limited, most of the insurance would be purchased from the government.

Although some reinsurance schemes along these lines have been examined by the FDIC, most recently in 1993, and were dismissed after the FDIC concluded that this market is not feasible, there is reason to be more optimistic today. Financial markets, in general, have become much more sophisticated in how they develop niche markets. For example, motivated by the events of September 11, 2001, the Terrorism Risk Insurance Act (TRIA), first passed in November 2002, offers federal reinsurance for qualifying losses from a terrorist attack. TRIA is a good place to start and includes industry loss triggers and government coverage of excess losses. These features help minimize the insurance industry's losses, yet also provide them with an incentive to monitor and reduce risks. While we believe that the insurance design would have to be somewhat different here, TRIA shows that co-insurance programs are not without precedent.

Specifically, in our private-public partnership, the securitizer would purchase a fraction of its insurance from a monoline insurance company and the rest from a newly formed government entity, which we will call the Government Mortgage Risk Insurance Corporation (GMRIC). As with terrorism risk insurance, the private insurance market would help to establish a market price for mortgage default risk. The newly formed GMRIC would charge a fee based on this market price. This would ensure that the government receives adequate compensation for the credit risk—a key difference with the precrisis approach.

The advantage of establishing a market price cannot be underestimated. While the public-private guarantee will ensure sufficient liquidity in the secondary market and lower mortgage rates, these rates will now reflect the true market and credit risk of the underlying mortgages. Investors will purchase MBS that reflect these rates and thus the price of the underlying mortgage insurance. Most important, because market prices will no longer be distorted, competing private markets will no longer be crowded out. Therefore, markets for MBS without guarantees will be free to develop. If enough liquidity can be sustained in these markets, investors will be able to move along the risk-return trade-off curve, private capital markets will grow, and the government will become less involved in mortgage finance.

While combining some of the advantages of the nationalization and privatization options just discussed, the hybrid option avoids the undesirable aspects of the pre-2008 public-private system. As in the privatization option, regulation would still need to be imposed both to prevent securitizers from bulking into large systemic entities that would pose the same risks as did Fannie Mae and Freddie Mac and to ensure that insurance companies that provide private insurance are well capitalized. The transitional issues would be handled the same way as in the private solution described above.

Here, we present some more specific details about how this private-public partnership would work:

1. The fraction of insurance that needs to be purchased from monoline insurance companies or mortgage insurance subsidiary units of larger financial institutions needs to be sufficient for the insurance companies to have enough of a stake to provide a liquid market and an efficient pricing mechanism—say, 25% for the purposes of this discussion. This 25% stake, however, needs to be sufficiently small so as not to create systemic-risk externalities in the private sector.
2. The government would be a silent partner in this effort, simply providing capital for the remaining 75% of the mortgage insurance and collecting fees on the 75%, albeit using a price determined from the mortgage insurance company's 25% stake. This government percentage could decline over time if it appeared that the private sector was capable of absorbing an increasing fraction of the guarantee activity.
3. A key feature of the private-public partnership structure is a credible resolution authority for the private mortgage insurance companies. The companies would be required to hold enough capital to weather a large, but not any, macroeconomic shock. Upon failure, the mortgage guarantees would be pari passu with the unsecured debt of the private companies. If MBS suffered losses and the companies failed, investors would receive the 75% coverage from the GMRIC and would be creditors of the private insurance companies for the remaining 25%.[5] This way, market discipline is restored to an extent because both creditors of the insurance

company and MBS investors are now liable for a fraction of the MBS losses.

4. Note that the insurance company might be a monoline, but could also be a subsidiary within a larger organization. If the latter, the subsidiary would have to be independently capitalized and ring-fenced and thus protected against losses at the parent company. In other words, the insurance subsidiary would be treated similarly to other insurance units, such as life insurance subsidiaries, that are housed within larger organizational forms and subject to its own resolution authority.
5. Capital requirement rules for investors in the MBS that are issued under the public-private partnership would need to be carefully designed in order to avoid a new round of regulatory arbitrage. Leading up to the financial crisis, GSE debt and guaranteed MBS were charged lower capital requirements. As described in chapter 1, this led to a vicious circle of financial institutions' originating GSE-conforming mortgages, financial institutions' providing debt financing for the GSEs to purchase these same mortgages and/or issue MBS, and then financial institutions' further levering up on these MBS. The result was an increasing interconnection between the banking sector and the GSEs, and greater leverage all around. Specifically, we propose that the MBS under the private-public partnership would get risk weights for capital that equal 75% of typical agency securities to reflect the government guarantee and 25% of the underlying rating (i.e., risk) of the mortgage insurance company.
6. The GMRIC would be a boring government-run public utility with the sole purpose of passively co-insuring the credit risk on conforming (core) mortgages. Explicitly barred from holding any mortgage-related assets, it could hold only Treasuries, which keep their value during crises. It would have no say over the composition of borrowers (e.g., fraction of low-income borrowers), other than a strict adherence to the definition of a conforming (core) mortgage. It would be tightly regulated by the FHFA. The GMRIC would be fully accounted for on the government budget.

Note that our hybrid solution is quite similar to what the Mortgage Bankers Association (MBA) has recently proposed.[6] They envision replacing the GSEs with two or three "mortgage credit guarantor entities" (MCGEs) that would guarantee timely payment of principal and interest on "core" mortgage loans—presumably, those defined as conventional conforming single-family and multifamily mortgages. These MCGEs would be new, private, monoline insurers that would own the mortgage loans and issue MBS against them. They would be financed by debt and equity and not carry any government guarantee. The MBS that they issue would be guaranteed by the full faith and credit of the U.S. government. The federal insurance fund (a role that could be assigned to Ginnie Mae) would receive a risk-based insurance fee from the MCGEs in return for this credit risk insurance.

It is not clear how the guarantee fee that the government receives would be set in the MBA proposal. As mentioned earlier, we view the most important element of a private-public partnership to be the market pricing of all of the guarantees. This is a substantial problem of the MBA proposal in our view. We also fear that only "two or three" MCGEs, which are subject to loan-level credit risk and would still be allowed to hold some mortgages in portfolio, would create new systemically risky institutions, which would need to be bailed out in the event of a major housing crisis.

A recent study by economists of the Federal Reserve Bank of New York also proposes a hybrid solution.[7] In it, the mortgage originators would form a private lender cooperative in order to securitize conforming mortgages. The cooperative would share the profits and the "normal losses" in proportion to the members' origination share. The losses arising from "tail risks"—rare events such as the one that we witnessed in 2008–9—would be borne by the government. In return for bearing the tail risk, the government would charge the cooperative a fee.

This proposal differs from ours in that the lenders would bear the first losses and the government would bear losses only in extreme events (although it is not clear what exactly constitutes an extreme event). This is similar in spirit to the aforementioned TRIA. Our proposal has a parallel loss-sharing arrangement. In an extreme housing crisis, the cooperative would lose all of its capital and would likely need to be bailed out by the government (unless it had a 100% capitalization). In that sense, it is like a private-sector GSE. Our proposal has investors in MBS that will potentially lose, say, 25% of their investment if the private insurer that they select goes bust and there is no recovery. This incentivizes the investor to do due diligence and the private-sector insurer to adhere to solid origination standards. Our proposal also has the advantage of firmly establishing a market price for the default risk, while it is not so obvious how the government would establish and enforce a fair tail-risk price. Market prices will in theory not crowd out other private-sector solutions, allowing for greater financial innovation.

8.3 NONCONFORMING MORTGAGES

The preceding proposals—whether nationalization, privatization, or our hybrid private-public partnership—deal with conforming mortgages. But there are a substantial number of mortgages that either are underwater or have mark-to-market loan-to-value ratios (LTVs) above the conforming limit of 80%. For example, as of the end of 2009, there were 47 million homeowners with a mortgage. A staggering 24 million (or 51%) had less than 25% equity, with 11.3 million of these having LTVs greater than 100% and another 2.3 million approaching negative equity.[8] Therefore, under the conforming mortgage proposals, almost 50% of the market would currently be precluded from any type of refinancing, thus increasing their mortgage costs and putting even greater pressure on the housing market.

Our suggestion in the previous section on the hybrid solution for the guarantee business could potentially be extended from conforming (core) mortgage loan pools to nonconforming loans (prime jumbo, Alt-A, and subprime). In other words, the GMRIC could potentially co-insure the default risk on some or all of the nonconforming market, alongside the private sector. One could argue that the GSEs have already been active in the jumbo market segment since 2008. Indeed, the conforming loan limit—the maximum size mortgage loans that Freddie and Fannie can purchase—was $417,000 nationwide in 2007. It then changed to a location-specific maximum between $417,000 and $729,750, depending on the cost of housing. This effectively constitutes a foray into jumbo lending for the GSEs.

One advantage of extending the hybrid market to nonconforming loans is that it may help to revitalize, or at least protect, the nonprime mortgage market, which has been anemic since the start of the financial crisis in 2007. The second, and main, advantage of such extension is that the government would receive compensation for the systematic credit risk that resides in nonconforming mortgages and which it ultimately bears anyway. As in the 2007–9 crisis, most of that default risk in the event of a major housing crisis is, in fact, concentrated in the nonprime mortgage segment.

Obviously, the price for guaranteeing the credit risk of such nonconforming mortgages will be substantially higher than for conforming mortgages. Because the co-insurance scheme should not involve any government subsidy, it may well turn out that the market price for this insurance proves prohibitively high so that (the riskiest) nonconforming mortgages are held by the banking sector or securitized in the private-label mortgage-backed securities (PLS) market without guarantees. However, if the private market sets the wrong insurance prices, the consequences are much more severe in terms of the moral hazard impact given the government involvement and given the highly risky nature of underlying mortgages. In fact, it may well not be desirable for society to stimulate noncore mortgage lending in any way or shape, as it may lead to a repeat of the excessive credit extension of the housing boom in 2000–6.

For these reasons, we do not feel that the public-private partnership is a viable option for the nonconforming mortgage market.[9] While some guarantees might be necessary initially to restore the mortgage market, it is clear to us that these guarantees should be focused on tightly underwritten core mortgages with the eventual goal of the government substantially reducing its role in mortgage finance. It seems that any proposal that would have the U.S. government co-insure all of the mortgage credit risk in the United States, or even all of the tail risk, would lead to an even bigger catastrophe than the one we just experienced.

The question is, What alternatives exist for the nonconforming mortgage market?

The only option appears to be the development, and most likely a slow one, of a private-sector mortgage lending market for nonconforming mortgages. This market in theory would consider and price in the loan's LTV, FICO score, and the borrower's income-to-mortgage-interest ratio, as well as intangible information. As in other countries, it may well be that this market is not securitized, and loans would be held on the balance sheet of financial institutions as whole loans. It may be, however, that simpler, more standardized structured finance products develop and at least some of these loans would therefore be packaged and sold off as MBS to the capital markets at large. In any event, if financial firms hold on to these loans, or purchase the MBS in the secondary market, these firms will need to be well capitalized and systemically less risky than other firms.

It is pie in the sky, however, to believe that systemic risk will not exist in the mortgage finance market and that financial institutions will not gradually build up this risk on their balance sheets. It is unavoidable. As a result, it is crucial that the external costs of systemic risk are internalized by each financial institution; otherwise, these institutions will have the incentive to take risks that are not borne just by the institution but instead by society as a whole. This means that systemically important financial firms that are active in holding nonconforming mortgages as whole loans or as MBS should be charged either higher capital requirements, concentration limits, or a systemic-risk "tax" in order to prevent them from accumulating too much systemic risk.[10]

Consider the most likely remedy: higher capital requirements. Whatever capital requirements are placed on one set of financial institutions—say banks and bank holding companies—it is important that the financing of riskier mortgages does not just move elsewhere in the shadow banking system.[11] In other words, the whole financial system must be looked at and treated in unison. In addition, without concentration limits or a systemic-risk tax, it is highly likely that nonconforming mortgage finance would just end up with financial firms that have government guarantees, such as FDIC-insured banks and too-big-to-fail institutions. As we have argued in the earlier chapters, the more guarantees that a firm receives, the lower are its costs of debt funding, which could lead to an alternative group of private GSE firms in the mortgage finance area.

Yale economist John Geanakoplos has argued that it is not possible to solve this problem at the institutional level—measuring leverage and then implementing capital requirements fairly across financial firms.[12] He argues instead that leverage should be legislated at the security level. This idea is tantamount to requiring a significant down payment or even banning nonconforming mortgages. We believe that an innovative way around this problem is that systemically risky firms could hold nonconforming mortgages but simultaneously would have to hold a position offsetting this risk—a so called "macro hedge." It would work as follows. For each dollar of nonconforming mortgage on the balance sheet, the firm would have a short position in an index of similarly risky MBS.[13]

Recently, President Obama signed the most comprehensive financial regulation since the Great Depression: the Dodd-Frank Act. What effect will it have on the market for nonconforming mortgages? The act can be evaluated in light of the distinction between legislating the systemic risk of financial institutions and placing restrictions at the mortgage level.

It is not clear at this stage how the Dodd-Frank Act will treat risky mortgages on the balance sheet in terms of systemic-risk contribution. But this aside, with respect to systemic risk, the act recognizes that systemic institutions must be subject to more stringent standards that should increase with the degree of systemic risk.[14] Moreover, these prudential standards cover the likely suspects, such as risk-based capital and liquidity requirements. While the devil is in the details, there is room to be skeptical. The rules will most likely end up following the latest Basel accords—we are now on Basel number 3—but some economists point to earlier Basel accords as partially responsible for the current financial crisis.[15]

Perhaps, the other way that the act, recognizing this point, deals with systemic risk is to try to end too-big-to-fail institutions by setting up a resolution authority. This is clearly a step in the right direction, but the authority is most likely inadequate for this purpose. Its preference is to put the institution through a receivership process, which is not a particularly credible way to ensure that systemic liabilities will be left unprotected in a crisis. A more transparent and predictable design would be one based on the bankruptcy code, possibly restructured to deal with the financial King Kongs.[16]

The Dodd-Frank Act, therefore, might be more successful at the individual asset level—in this case, regulating nonconforming mortgages. The act implements two major pieces of legislation on this front. The first is that, in order to align incentives better on the underwriting front, securitizers of mortgage loans must hold at least 5% of the credit risk—that is, they must have "skin in the game."[17] There is an exemption for "qualified residential mortgages," which has yet to be defined, but most likely means conforming mortgages. While aligning incentives is an admirable goal for the nonconforming mortgage market, as we have argued elsewhere, it was probably not the problem in the financial crisis. As described in chapter 3, no one can accuse the Godzilla GSEs and their King Kong too-big-to-fail private counterparts from not having had enough skin in the game (but, of course, they did not have enough capital to cover their skin).

The second route is to rely on a consumer finance protection bureau (CFPB), housed at the Fed, to monitor and create rules for the nonconforming mortgage market. While some observers worry about the potential for overreaching, at least with respect to mortgages, the CFPB is in the spirit of limiting the nonconforming mortgage market. Specifically, Title XIV of the act, Mortgage Reform and Anti-Predatory Lending Act, attempts to do this by applying minimum underwriting standards for mortgages, including prohibitions on steering incentives for mortgage brokers (i.e., payments to brokers for selling specific types of loans); restrictions on prepayment penalties; restrictions on high-cost mortgages; and a requirement that lenders make a "reasonable and good faith determination" that borrowers have a "reasonable ability to repay" the loan that they are taking out.[18] Moreover, the act goes on to describe the basis for determining whether the borrower can pay, including typical features such as credit history, income, and their current obligations, as well as income verification and the type of loan if nonstandard (such as variable rate, interest-only, negative amortization).

In light of all of the difficulties in trying to manage the mortgage risk at the financial institution level, it is hard to argue that a reduction in predatory lending and higher underwriting standards would not improve the securitization process. But it should be understood that these provisions will almost certainly reduce the availability of mortgage credit and/or increase its price. Nevertheless, there is little doubt that some types of nonconforming mortgages could be economically viable, even at higher mortgage rates. We believe that it would be a shame if the best practices of the subprime market did not reemerge—for example, providing credit to the self-employed who may fall outside the scope of conforming mortgages. Direct stipulation of underwriting standards might straitjacket originators, who through innovative contractual and monitoring mechanisms or simply different credit terms, such as requiring a higher down payment, could provide prudent mortgage finance to niche markets.

Nevertheless, almost surely the Dodd-Frank Act necessitates a smaller mortgage finance market, pushing potential homeowners towards the rental market. And this may not be all that bad. The next chapter discusses the economics of home ownership and, more specifically, the large number of subsidies that are provided by the U.S. government to this market.

9

CHASING THE DRAGON

> In this context, it's especially disturbing that the Bush administration has announced that it is cutting back Section 8 housing vouchers, which provide rental assistance to low income families, while easing restrictions on mortgage loans. Low-income families will now be able to get subsidized mortgage loans through the Federal Housing Administration that are equal to 103% of the purchase price of a home. Home ownership can sometimes be a ticket to the middle class, but buying homes at bubble-inflated prices may saddle hundreds of thousands of poor families with an unmanageable debt burden.
>
> —*Dean Baker,* Nation, *August 16, 2004*

In 1916 at the University of Frankfurt in Germany, scientists Martin Freund and Edmund Speyer developed the drug, oxycodone, as an alternative to heroin, which had been branded, marketed, and sold from 1898 to 1910 by the drug company Bayer as a painkiller. As an opioid painkiller, the expectation was that oxycodone would be a prescription for severe pain, yet would have none of the severe consequences of heroin such as its long-lasting nature, its addictive impact on the brain, and its possible deadly effect if taken in excessive quantity.

In many ways, the development of oxycodone has been a resounding success. It is not only formulated as a single product but combined with numerous over-the-counter painkillers. The products include such familiar names as OxyContin, Percocet, Depalgos, and Percodan, among others. From approximately 11 tons of production in 1998, it grew sevenfold to 75 tons by 2007, approximately 80% of which services the U.S. market.

The problem is that, if oxycodone is not taken rarely and then carefully in moderation, it is highly addictive with almost 100% surety—more so than almost any narcotic, alcohol, or tobacco. With each prescription, the individual needs a little more next time for the same sense of satisfaction—so-called chasing the dragon—leading to a downward spiral. Going cold turkey does not work well as the side effects of withdrawal are severe. And, unfortunately, the United States as a whole has become addicted to painkillers. In the summer of 2010, the U.S. Department of Health and Human Services' Substance Abuse and Mental Health Services Administration reported that abuse of opioid painkillers like oxycodone had risen more than 400% over the past decade with no sign of abatement.

In a similar way, the United States is addicted to home ownership, and there is perhaps no better example than the tax credits provided by the U.S. government for home buying during the financial crisis.[1]

Initially put forth in July 2008 with the Housing and Economic Recovery Act, first-time home buyers were to receive a credit of $7,500 for purchases between April 2008 and July 2009. Taxpayers, however, were required to repay the credit over a 15-year period—the equivalent of a mortgage finance "small Percocet dose." As it wore off, and the housing pain had not disappeared, some six months later, in February 2009, the Economic Stimulus bill increased the credit to $8,000 and dropped the repayment requirement—a step up in its "dose." And then in

November 2009, Congress extended the credit an additional five months and now included not only credit for first-time home buyers but also a $6,500 credit for homeowners who were relocating—yet another increase in the "dose."

The housing market felt much better. And while the government was patting itself on the back for easing the housing pain and stabilizing markets, the tax credits expired and, in July 2010, sales of new homes sank to the lowest point since the 1960s, when the government started keeping records. Now, again, there is discussion of what to do next.

Like addiction to painkillers, these remedies provide short-term "benefits" against increasing costs in the long-term. Which solution lawmakers ultimately choose for the future of the GSEs depends intimately on how they answer the much deeper question of how much society should promote and subsidize home ownership.

9.1 THE ECONOMICS OF SUBSIDIZING HOME OWNERSHIP

In a November 3, 2009, report titled "An Overview of Federal Support for Housing," the Congressional Budget Office (CBO) estimated that the federal government provided approximately $300 billion in subsidies to housing and mortgage markets in 2009. As a comparison, the much maligned farm subsidies and support for energy initiatives each receive approximately $20 billion per year. The degree of support for home ownership is staggering.

In the United States, home ownership in particular is stimulated by four main government policies: the home-mortgage interest rate and property tax deductibility, the tax exemption of rental income enjoyed implicitly from home ownership, the exemption from income tax of capital gains on the sale of owner-occupied houses, and the lower interest rates that are enjoyed thanks to government support of the GSEs. In addition, there is a myriad of other programs, such as the reduced interest cost on mortgages insured by the Federal Housing Administration (FHA) and the Department of Veterans Affairs (the former Veterans Administration, or VA), tax credits for home purchases, favorable funding from the Federal Home Loan Bank System (as well as FDIC deposit insurance) for thrifts and other depository institutions that invest in real estate, and mandates for thrifts to invest in residential mortgages. Finally, there are programs that stimulate housing more broadly, such as rent subsidy programs, subsidies for the construction of rental housing (e.g., low-income housing tax credit), and direct provision of public housing by the government.

"Too much is never enough" is a reasonable summary of this array of housing policies.

As the CBO report outlined, these programs are expensive: the current home mortgage interest rate deductibility, for example, will cost $105 billion in lost federal tax revenue in fiscal year 2011. Property tax exemption, exclusion of implicit rental income,

and exclusion of capital gains taxes upon sale of the house will cost an additional $92 billion in 2011.

These programs come at a cost that is overlooked in the public debate: they make housing relatively cheaper and other goods relatively more expensive. This, in turn, leads to more consumption of housing, more investment in housing and construction, but less business investment and less consumption of nonhousing goods and services. The consensus among economists is that investment in residential real estate is substantially less productive (at the margin) than is capital investment by businesses outside the real estate sector (e.g., plant, equipment, inventories), investment in social infrastructure capital (e.g., highways, bridges, airports, water and sewage systems), or investment in human capital (e.g., more and better education and training). In other words, every additional dollar that is spent on residential construction instead of on business or other investment reduces economic growth. Careful research has found that all of the incentives for more house has led to a housing stock that is 30% (!) larger than would be the case if all of the incentives were absent, and that U.S. GDP is 10% smaller than it could be.[2] The United States simply has too much house!

The analogy to drug addiction is not without merit.

Many politicians on the left and on the right equate reducing these housing subsidies to political suicide. After all, many believe that these policies are at the heart of the social contract with America and that they are therefore untouchable. Conventional wisdom has it that home ownership confers such benefits as good citizens, stable neighborhoods, strong communities, and—of course—personal wealth accumulation.[3] This "conventional wisdom" has met not only with a massive destruction of home equity in recent years but also with mixed reviews in academic research.[4] Nevertheless, housing subsidies have been and still are *the* policy tool of choice for combating income inequality, which has been on the rise in the United States since the 1970s.

However, research has shown that these policies predominantly benefit middle- to upper-income groups rather than the low-income group. One recent research paper specifically on the GSE subsidy by Jeske, Krueger, and Mitman finds that its effect is a *loss in overall welfare and an increase in inequality*.[5] Their model indicates that low-income households would be willing to pay 0.3% of lifetime consumption to live in a world without the GSE subsidy. The wealthy, instead, benefit from the subsidy. Jeske et al. find that the subsidy may not even be that powerful for increasing home ownership because, by stimulating construction, it also makes rental housing cheaper and more attractive for low-income, low-asset households.

In earlier research, academics have reached a similar conclusion regarding the home mortgage interest deduction. It too is regressive, benefiting high-income, high-asset households the most. Upper-income households are more likely to itemize on their income tax returns and to have higher marginal tax rates (which is what makes the mortgage interest and property tax deductions more valuable), and they are more likely to buy higher-priced houses (which would involve larger mortgages and hence more benefits). Gervais calculates that abolishing the deduction would benefit the bottom 20% nearly six times more than the top 20% of the income distribution.[6] Abolishing the tax advantage from owning would benefit everyone somewhat (in the long run) because it would lead to a larger business capital stock (and possibly more social infrastructure and more human capital) and a smaller housing capital stock, which would positively affect economic growth. More recent work by Poterba and Sinai estimates that the benefits from the home mortgage interest deduction for the average home-owning household that earns between $40,000 and $75,000 are *one-tenth* of the benefits that accrue to the average home-owning household earning more than $250,000.[7]

The current policies do not discriminate between first-time home purchasers and households simply wanting to buy larger houses or (for the GSE subsidies) even second homes. Rather, the policies promote larger home purchases. Census data show that the square footage of new houses grew by about 50% between the mid-1970s and the mid-2000s. Although some of this increase surely reflected growing household incomes, some of the increase also surely reflected the growing value of the subsidy advantages for buying larger houses. Similarly, studies show that U.S. home sizes are substantially above those in Western European countries that have similar or only slightly lower household incomes—and that even the home sizes of lower-income owner-occupiers in the United States are well above the *averages* for Western Europe.

Finally, the deduction encourages people to borrow as much as possible. Encouraging household leverage does not strike us as the best possible policy. Thus, ironically, although one of the motives for encouraging home ownership was to provide households with a means of building wealth, the process of making borrowing cheap and easy encouraged these households to borrow excessively, and then to borrow again if interest rates declined and/or their house value increased. In the process, they reduce the amount of net equity that they might otherwise build in their home. The metaphor of the refinancing household's using their home as an ATM to finance consumption was a strong one in the mid-2000s. And, of course, the excessive leverage and the cashing out of equity meant that the declines in housing prices after mid-2006 caused more houses to be "underwater," where the value of the house was less than the outstanding principal on the enlarged mortgage. And, in turn, this meant more instances where households defaulted on their mortgages.

There is no social purpose that is served by such "more house" investments—a fifth bedroom rather than four, a fourth bathroom rather than three, a half acre of land rather than a third of an acre—and no social purpose that is served by excessive leverage.

In sum, in addition to reducing the overall size of the pie, the policy of fighting income inequality by subsidizing home ownership redistributes the pie to the wrong people. Clearly, the housing policy of the past is misguided, and there is an urgent need to think of more effective ways to halt the increase in income inequality.

It should be clear, however, what purpose is served by the household leverage that is provided in the form of off-budget guarantees through Fannie and Freddie. This is what so far allowed successive presidential administrations to encourage ever-larger short-term consumption and spending during their tenures. It might seem odd that in a game between two political parties to get to the seat, both would agree on a strategy to promote housing finance at successively higher levels over time. The game, however, is not between the two parties but between each current administration and the future ones (and ultimately current and future taxpayers). No president would want to shut down or bring onto the federal budget Fannie's and Freddie's debt or guarantees—until they have to be honored. Doing so would seriously alter the shape of that administration's fiscal budget and force it to make hard choices that would produce long-term gains that would accrue only to future administrations. Instead, as long as possible, it would be better to let households spend more on housing, passing on the problem of dealing with housing guarantees to the next government, and so on. And while each presidential administration is working its way through its term, aided by Fannie's and Freddie's balance sheets and off-balance-sheet guarantees, the competitive landscape of the financial sector is altered as they enter more mortgage markets, which contributes to a downward spiral of lending standards, excess leverage, and an unsustainable bubble in housing prices and construction.

In many ways, this is the ultimate Ponzi scheme of all. It reflects a deep failure of a society's ability to govern its own governments. That in turn is generally a sign of poor quality of institutions. In the emerging markets, economists have generally argued this has to do with legal institutions such as the rule of law, creditor rights, and the protection of minority investors. In this case, it is the extent of involvement of state-backed enterprises, Fannie and Freddie, in private business. Ironically, it is another presidential administration that must take the steps to reform them. But we must guide the reforms to take a shape such that some future administration's desire to restart the Ponzi scheme can be kept in check.

9.2 SOLUTIONS TO THE HOME OWNERSHIP ISSUE

9.2.1 Lessons from Others

We now return to the question of whether a government presence in mortgage markets is necessary for social goals relating to housing, even if these goals were desirable for some reason as government objectives. According to our analysis in chapter 7, the answer seems to be a resounding no.

Despite their substantially lower level of government involvement, other countries have been as successful as the United States in promoting home ownership and affordable housing. On the basis of the cross-country evidence, it seems fair to conclude that there is no obvious link between the extent of government support and key indicators of success in housing policy, such as the home ownership rate and housing affordability. The international evidence that we presented in chapter 7 lends further credibility to our recommendation of reduced support for home ownership in the United States. And the fact that government involvement, in fact, contributed to the boom and bust cycle makes the case for reduced support even stronger. As we have noted before, house prices fell more in the United States than in most other countries, the financial crisis was deeper, and the macroeconomy contracted more sharply than in many other economies.

There is perhaps some link between government support through the GSEs (through their guarantee function rather than through their investment function) and the emergence of the 30-year prepayable fixed-rate mortgage (FRM) as the standard mortgage contract in the United States.[8] Without well-developed secondary markets for mortgages, it is hard to sustain this mortgage product. The fact that this product thrives elsewhere only in Australia and Canada, which also have well-developed securitization markets, is a testament to this point. Some have argued that a larger fraction of FRMs has the benefit of macroeconomic and monetary stability, as it makes households' balance sheets less vulnerable to interest rate changes. To the extent that U.S. households have come to know and love this product, any GSE reform should consider the importance of maintaining a strong securitization market so as to preserve the availability of a long-term fixed-rate mortgage product. (However, the issue of whether FRMs should allow prepayments without fees is a separate matter.) Even if there is a smaller proportion of FRMs in the steady state as a result of reduced GSE involvement, in the transition these mortgages will continue to be the most important part of the mortgage market. The private-public partnership we proposed in the previous chapter would be one way to provide such support to the securitization market.

There also seems to be a link between the recourse laws and mortgage foreclosures. Because U.S. households are able to walk away from their mortgage debt more easily, the United States faces a much deeper foreclosure crisis than do other countries. Strengthening and facilitating recourse reduces the credit risk in the mortgage market—arguably substantially. On the one hand, this may lead to more prudent borrowing on the part of the households and better allocation of credit in the economy. It could lower mortgage rates for all, as lenders pass on the gain of lower foreclosures to all borrowers. On the other hand, being able to walk away from a mortgage offers households in trouble a fresh start, which may be desirable from a risk-sharing perspective and may promote more labor market mobility. On balance, mopping up seems much harder than saving for the rainy day. The stability of mortgage finance may be substantially enhanced by a strengthening of the recourse feature for mortgage lenders in the United States.

9.2.2 Transition

The GSEs should get out of the business of promoting home ownership for low-income households and underserved regions. As we mentioned earlier, Freddie and Fannie have mission quotas for lending in underserved areas and to households with incomes below the local median income. We strongly recommend abolishing these quotas because they have contributed to the increasing riskiness of the GSE portfolios. Because they constrained the GSEs in terms of the portion of the company's mortgage purchases that went to a specific set of borrowers, they mechanically forced the GSEs to take on a large fraction of risky loans as the economic situation of these households deteriorated. Furthermore, the consensus among academics is that the affordable housing goals have not substantially increased home ownership among low-income families.[9]

We believe that whatever decision is made about the future of the GSEs, the current joint mandate of making secondary mortgage markets liquid and well functioning and of promoting access to mortgage credit by underserved groups of regions are mutually incompatible. As described earlier, the current approach of government intervention through the GSEs—to keep mortgage interest rates artificially low for all households—is both too expensive and ineffective.

Instead, the policy objective of promoting and subsidizing low-income home ownership should be the exclusive domain of the Federal Housing Administration and its securitizer Ginnie Mae. These institutions have the expertise with low-income mortgage insurance and securitization and are much better suited to perform the targeted role of helping the underserved income groups or regions. Ginnie Mae, for example, runs an efficient securitization business, with no retained portfolio, little risk, and a small staff. Such a focused approach would be not only more effective but also much more transparent, with its costs and benefits in plain sight and part of the government budget.

Having lost market share to subprime lenders and to the GSEs during the boom, the FHA has filled the void after the collapse of private-sector lending and the GSEs. Rather than continuing to expand the market share of FHA, now is the time to delineate which households deserve mortgage support through the FHA. As a general principal, mortgage assistance programs should be targeted more toward low-income households.

Whenever possible, home ownership policy should aim at helping potential homeowners without promoting excessive leverage. Rental subsidies, such as the HUD rental voucher program, may be a more cost effective way to help low-income households than are poorly conceived ownership stimulus or mortgage guarantees. Finally, federal housing policy would benefit from streamlining and consolidating the myriad programs that support low-income housing and benefit from modernization so as to execute its mission effectively.

While our focus has been on single-family mortgages, the GSEs have also played an important role in financing multifamily mortgages in the United States These multifamily mortgages are important for the creation of rental housing. Currently, the

GSEs hold 35% of total outstanding multifamily mortgage debt and are providing nearly 90% of all mortgage capital to the market. The majority of these mortgages are held in portfolio, either because it is profitable to do so (similar to the single-family mortgage argument that we made before) or because they are harder to securitize than are single-family housing. We propose that support for the multifamily market segment be transferred to the FHA and be confined to low-income housing. The standardization efforts of the GSEs should be preserved so that the private sector can become a larger multifamily player.

One fear of reducing the blanket housing subsidies that are offered through the GSEs is that households will face steeply higher mortgage interest rates, which in turn will trigger a decline in housing markets. New research by Favilukis, Ludvigson, and Van Nieuwerburgh and Glaeser, Gottlieb, and Gyourko shows that the link between interest rates and house prices may be weaker than is conventionally assumed.[10] This implies that the impact of policies that reduce housing subsidies may not be as dramatic as feared.

9.3 WHAT ABOUT THE FEDERAL HOME LOAN BANK SYSTEM?

Although we have mentioned the Federal Home Loan Bank System as another sizable GSE a number of times in this book, Fannie Mae and Freddie Mac have been our major focus of attention. Nevertheless, the FHLB System deserves attention as well—perhaps most importantly because fixing Fannie and Freddie will not suffice if some other GSE takes on their functions (even though that is not on the table just as yet).

This risk is serious with respect to the FHLB System. This system is another GSE—in fact, an early GSE formed in the 1930s—that was originally designed to support housing via the S&Ls. After 1989 the system expanded support to almost all depository institutions, with its mission expanded to helping "community development." And, in the crisis of 2007–9, the system became a significant lender of last resort to depository institutions that were experiencing problems with their mortgage portfolios (including institutions that eventually failed, such as Washington Mutual and Countrywide).

The FHLB System thus far has not generated the financial trauma that has been caused by Fannie and Freddie. Although some of the individual banks in the 12-bank FHLB System have had financial difficulties, none has approached insolvency; and the joint-and-several-liability structure of the system's debt obligations reduces the likelihood that a federal government rescue will be needed.

Nevertheless, the FHLB System presents the same worrisome clash of social goals (supporting housing and, more recently, supporting community development) and private ownership. We believe that the FHLB System's basic role as a wholesale bank for its constituent financial institutions can be served by a wholly private entity that does not have the implicit subsidy of the GSE status. We are also worried that a GSE-based FHLB System might become the vehicle for a new expansion of housing subsidies. Hence, we recommend its transformation into a wholly private structure.

More generally, privatization of GSEs in some cases and the evolution of others into public-private partnerships with a limited life-span for the public arm could pave the way for more balanced government intervention and sustainable growth in housing markets.

EPILOGUE

The difficulty lies, not in the new ideas,
but in escaping from the old ones.

—John Maynard Keynes in The General Theory of Employment, Interest and Money *(1936)*

On November 6, 1961, in the Sahara desert in Algeria, a pipeline from a natural gas well ripped open, leading to a gas fire that was 750 feet high. Nicknamed the Devil's Cigarette Lighter, and fueled by 550 million cubic feet of gas a day, it burned for six months without any end in sight. The heat was so intense that anything within one-half mile, including the desert sand, melted.

Then a Texan named Red Adair showed up. Red and his team dug deep down in the sand until a water source was reached. Using this new found water supply, they drenched the surrounding area for weeks upon weeks, thus cooling the area down. Then one day, fully covered in his fire suit that had been sprayed with water, Red calmly rode a bulldozer into the fire's perimeter, placed drums carrying 750 pounds of nitroglycerine, and pulled away, igniting a massive explosion. The explosion successfully blew out the fire. It is generally considered the greatest achievement in the history of fighting oil well fires.

The financial sector has its own version of the Devil's Cigarette Lighter, and it is the government-sponsored enterprises (GSEs), notably Fannie Mae and Freddie Mac, with their unstable mix of capitalist profit taking and socialized risk.

While no one disagrees with the idea of reforming the GSEs, it seems that the proposals for housing finance reform that are emerging from various industry groups do not represent a tectonic shift in thinking about government's role in housing finance. For that matter, politicos are still mentioning the public mission of affordable housing and GSEs in the same breath.

Regulators and policy makers need to stop dancing around the issue of what to do with the GSEs. A little less Fred Astaire and a little more Red Adair is needed.[1]

Of course, critics will argue that, without the support of the GSEs, the cost of obtaining mortgages will be that much higher, effectively shutting out a large number of potential home buyers, and the liquidity of the secondary mortgage market will be significantly impaired. In fact, in an interview with the *Financial Times* that appeared on August 12, 2010, legendary bond investor Bill Gross of Pimco stated: "Without a government guarantee, as a private investor, I'd require borrowers to put at least 30 per cent down, and most first-time homebuyers can't afford that."

But if mortgage lenders and securitizers cannot issue and securitize mortgages without full government backing, then this says more about the current business model of mortgage securitization than anything else. If we really think that the only source of capital is the government, we will have implicitly socialized the mortgage financial system.

It is certainly true that the vast expansion of mortgage finance could not have taken place without the involvement of the GSEs. But why was this expansion necessarily a good thing? The current administration is desperately trying to keep the housing market afloat, even though all economic signs point in the opposite direction. The tale of this financial crisis is that homeowners, mortgage lenders, securitizers, and investors in mortgage-backed securities all took advantage of the freebies thrown at them either directly or indirectly by the GSEs and are now drowning in debt and crying foul that the gravy train is over.

Of course, the creative destructive nature of capitalism can solve this problem. Once the creditors of mortgage lenders get hit, and investors in mortgage-backed securities lose, market discipline will come back to the mortgage finance sector. Mortgage lenders will change their behavior and focus on borrower quality, and investors will audit these lenders and once again measure and price aggregate credit risk. As in other parts of the world, lower loan-to-value ratios (i.e., larger down payments) and stronger recourse for lenders will reduce the amount of mortgage default risk in the economy; and borrowers will choose adjustable-rate mortgages if the cost of fixed-rate mortgages becomes too high. All of this will lead to a private and more efficient level of risk sharing in the mortgage finance market. The reform of mortgage finance will end up being mostly organic and not require the heavy hand of government.

Nevertheless, there still might exist the market failure of systemic risk to the extent that individual financial firms do not bear all of the costs of lending, guaranteeing, or investing in the systemically risky housing market. The combination of having the government provide capital side by side with firms that offer mortgage guarantees and yet getting compensated on the basis of the private price of guarantees is one pragmatic compromise to address this issue. But limited government involvement of even this sort must be tightly ring-fenced to the relatively high-quality mortgages, and private provision of guarantees to the low-quality mortgages must be reasonably competitive and well capitalized at all times, lest new too-big-too-fail firms are created.

The temptation to opt for cheap housing credit is as irresistible for low-income households as it is for the government. However, it has proved woefully inadequate as a social policy tool to fight the increasing income inequality and redistributed wealth toward the rich. Ultimately, any policy that is not aimed directly at promoting economic growth by and large makes things worse. Government support of housing markets and institutions is a case in point.

APPENDIX

TIMELINE OF U.S. HOUSING FINANCE MILESTONES

Year/Act	Critical Reform or Event for Housing Finance
1932: Federal Home Loan Bank (FHLB) Act	Creation of an early government-sponsored enterprise (GSE): a system of 12 FHLBs to borrow at low rates in markets and lend to mortgage-lenders
"New Deal": 1933 Home Owners Loan Act (HOLA) and 1934 National Housing Act (NHA)	Creation of the Federal Housing Administration (FHA) that offered mortgage insurance to lenders on qualified mortgages
1938	Creation of the National Mortgage Association (NMA) of Washington, which changed its name to the Federal National Mortgage Association (FNMA)—"Fannie Mae"— authorized to borrow in capital markets and buy FHA-insured mortgages
1944: The Servicemen's Readjustment Act ("GI Bill of Rights")	Authorized the Veterans Administration (VA) to offer mortgage insurance (similar to FHA's) to veterans
1948	Fannie Mae gained the authority to buy the VA-insured mortgages
1954: The Federal National Mortgage Association Charter Act of 1954 (a part of the Housing Act of 1954)	Clarified Fannie Mae's status as a government agency, stipulated that it was exempt from state and local income taxes, provided for the Federal Reserve Banks to perform various services for Fannie Mae, and specified that Fannie Mae was to provide "special assistance" for certain kinds of mortgages, a precursor to the "mission" regulation of 1990s and 2000s

Year/Act	Critical Reform or Event for Housing Finance
1968: The Housing and Urban Development (HUD) Act	Converted Fannie Mae into a private company, with shares listed on the New York Stock Exchange, HUD retained some regulatory powers over Fannie Mae, and the president of the United States continued to have powers to appoint five of Fannie Mae's board members
1968–70: HUD Act	Creation of the Government National Mortgage Association (GNMA, or "Ginnie Mae") within HUD as an agency that would securitize FHA- and VA-insured mortgages; issuance of the first Ginnie Mae mortgage-backed securities (MBS) in 1970
1970: The Emergency Home Finance Act	Creation of the Federal Home Loan Mortgage Corporation ("Freddie Mac"), owned by the FHLB system, to buy and securitize mortgages from the S&Ls; issuance of Freddie Mac's first MBS in 1971
1970–80: HUD and the Federal Home Loan Bank Board	Fannie Mae authorized to purchase mortgages that were not insured by FHA or VA; both Fannie Mae and Freddie Mac restricted in size of mortgages they could purchase for holding or securitizing; "conforming loan limits" progressively revised upward over time
1980s: The Secondary Mortgage Market Enhancement Act of 1984	The maturity mismatch of the S&L industry and the high interest rate environment of the late 1970s and early 1980s led the "President's Commission on Housing" in 1982 to call for deregulation of mortgage banking and increased role for capital markets in secondary market for mortgages
1989: The Financial Institutions Reform, Recovery, and Enforcement Act (FIRREA)	Fundamentally established Fannie Mae and Freddie Mac as parallel GSEs, with similar structures, privileges, responsibilities, and limitations; lodged prudential regulation with HUD to ensure their solvency

Year/Act	Critical Reform or Event for Housing Finance
1992: The Federal Housing Enterprises Financial Safety and Soundness Act (FHEFSSA)	Creation of the Office of Federal Housing Enterprise Oversight (OFHEO), which was lodged in HUD, as prudential regulator of the GSEs; specified a risk-based capital regulatory regime but with more generous terms than for private financial firms
1992: FHEFSSA	Specified for the first time a set of "mission goals" for the GSEs to support housing for low- and moderate-income households, as well as a special "affordable goal" and attention to "underserved areas" (formerly inner-city areas), effectively giving the GSEs a mandate to purchase low-quality mortgages
1992–2003	Steady increase in the proportion of GSE mortgage purchases mandated to serve the affordable housing goals
2003–4	Accounting scandals at Freddie Mac and Fannie Mae lead OFHEO to impose restrictions on leverage and size of balance sheets but without any limit on MBS guarantee business
2003–7: "Race to the bottom"	Non-GSE MBS (privately securitized) grew from 12% to 38% of originations; GSE profitability (in return on equity terms) eroded while that of investment banks (and their leverage too) skyrocketed; GSE and private-label MBS both grew substantially with general deterioration of lending and underwriting standards
2007–8	At the advent of the crisis, the FHLB System becomes the "lender of next-to-last resort" for commercial banks and thrifts, increasing its lending and assets to $1.3 trillion, exceeding the individual on-balance-sheet positions of either Fannie Mae or Freddie Mac

Year/Act	Critical Reform or Event for Housing Finance
July 2008: The Housing and Economic Recovery (HERA) Act	Fannie Mae's and Freddie Mac's share valuations collapse with imminent bankruptcy; the U.S. Treasury granted emergency powers under the HERA to deal with Fannie's and Freddie's problems; and HERA raised the Treasury's debt ceiling by $800 billion, to have the flexibility to support the GSEs
September 7, 2008	The GSEs are placed in government "conservatorships" with a line of credit of up to $100 billion each for Fannie Mae and Freddie Mac
2009	The Treasury first increases its commitment to $200 billion for Fannie Mae and Freddie Mae each in May 2009, then quietly removes the ceiling on the bailout altogether on Christmas Eve 2009, with a promise to make up any further negative net worth in 2010, 2011, and 2012
January 2009–May 2010	The Federal Reserve doubles its balance sheet via "quantitative easing" linked to GSE securities: $1,250 billion of GSE MBS and $172 billion of their debt
August 2010	GSEs run cumulative (negative net worth) losses of close to $150 billion, projected to double the loss with a worst-case estimate of $1 trillion; Obama administration holds a "conference" to assess possible proposals for GSE reforms

NOTES

CHAPTER 1: *Feeding the Beast*

[1] The process described in the text is conceptually the easiest way to understand what happens in a securitization, and it is the basis for some securitizations. More common, however, is a "swap" arrangement, whereby the GSE will swap the securities for the mortgages from the originator. The originator can then decide whether to hold the securities or to sell them in the secondary market. Similarly, when the GSE wants to hold mortgages in its portfolio, it most often buys back its own MBS from the secondary market; once the GSE possesses its own MBS, in essence it just owns the underlying mortgages.

[2] There will be some normal, background level of prepayment that is driven by household occupants who choose to move because of new job offers in a different city, because of changes in family size, or because of the households' changed economic circumstances. But, on top of this background rate, the ease of prepayment means that when interest rates decrease, mortgage borrowers will often refinance their mortgage at the lower rates, or households find that changed circumstances make selling their existing house (and repaying the mortgage) and buying another house more attractive—which means that the investor will not get the capital gain but instead will simply get the principal back,

but at a time when reinvestment possibilities are less attractive (because of the lower prevailing interest rates). In essence, prepayments speed up just when investors wish that they would slow down. Conversely, when interest rates rise, prepayments for refinancing will disappear, and even normal prepayments will slow down, and the investor experiences an even larger loss of value, because this lower-interest security now has a longer expected life. In essence, prepayments slow down just when investors wish that they would speed up.

[3] In other words, the famous Modigliani and Miller theorem of corporate finance that a firm's cost of capital should be invariant to its mix of debt and equity is clearly violated in the case of the GSEs because the more debt that they have relative to equity, the more that they can exploit the value of government guarantees. Franco Modigliani and Merton Miller, "The Cost of Capital, Corporation Finance and the Theory of Investment," *American Economic Review* 48 (3, 1958): 261–97.

[4] The savings and loan industry had largely avoided dealing with Fannie Mae; the S&L industry saw Fannie Mae as largely a vehicle to which mortgage companies (which came to be known as "mortgage banks," even though they weren't depository institutions) could sell mortgages that they had originated. The S&L industry lobbied Congress for a secondary mortgage institution that would be "theirs." In 1970 the Congress complied and created a charter for the Federal Home Loan Mortgage Corporation (FHLMC, which subsequently acquired the nickname "Freddie Mac").

[5] Ralph Nader, "How Fannie and Freddie Influence the Political Process," chapter 6 of *Serving Two Masters, Yet Out of Control: Fannie Mae and Freddie Mac*, edited by Peter Wallison (Washington, DC: AEI Press, 2001).

[6] This description is taken from Bethany McLean, "The Fall of Fannie Mae," *Fortune*, January 24, 2005.

[7] It should be noted, however, that because house prices increased over the 1995–2006 period, the collateral underlying this credit numerator increased in value, therefore decreasing the overall credit risk. However, as chapter 2 shows, the risk profile of these mortgages was also increasing over this period, thus mitigating this house price effect.

[8] Using an alternative approach based on options pricing, economists Deborah Lucas and Robert McDonald report a somewhat smaller value of $28 billion, though a recent update by the authors indicates that this value can increase with more realistic modeling. Of some interest, they show a value-at-risk at the 5% level for Fannie Mae (Freddie Mac) of $165 billion ($112 billion), eerily close to their losses in the current crisis if one is to believe the CBO estimates. Deborah Lucas and Robert McDonald, "An Options-Based Approach to Evaluating the Risk of Fannie Mae and Freddie Mac," *Journal of Monetary Economics* 53 (1, 2006,): 155–76, and "Valuing Government Guarantees: Fannie and Freddie Revisited," in *Measuring and Managing Federal Financial Risk*, edited by Deborah Lucas (Chicago: University of Chicago Press, 2010), pp. 131–54.

[9] Speech at the Conference on Housing, Mortgage Finance, and the Macroeconomy, Federal Reserve Bank of Atlanta, Atlanta, Georgia, dedicated to the theme of government-sponsored enterprises: http://www.federalreserve.gov/boarddocs/speeches/2005/20050519/.

CHAPTER 2: *Ticking Time Bomb*

[1] Within these mission goals, there were also so-called subgoals that stipulate the fraction of the goal that must be achieved through new home purchases, as opposed to through mortgage refinancing.

[2] *Housing and Community Development Act of 1992*, Title XIII, "Government Sponsored Enterprises," Sec. 1354 "Review of Underwriting Guidelines."

[3] See Brent W. Ambrose, Kenneth Temkin, and Thomas G. Thibodeau, "An Analysis of the Effects of the GSE Affordable Goals on Low- and Moderate-Income Families ," U.S. Department of Housing and Urban Development, Office of Policy Development and Research, 2002.

[4] As mentioned above, the GSEs generally required loans with LTVs > 80% to have private mortgage insurance. An important point, however, is that while private mortgage insurance helps insulate some of the GSE losses from a defaulted mortgage, the high LTVs also make default more likely. As is well documented, mortgage defaults usually create dead-weight losses that are associated with spillover effects in the neighborhood, disinvestment in the property, etc.

[5] See a detailed analysis by Ed Pinto, available at http://www.aei.org/docLib/Pinto-High-LTV-Subprime-Alt-A.pdf.

[6] The Fair Isaac Corporation—FICO—provides an analysis of the creditworthiness of an individual by looking at a variety of factors, including payment history, debt ratio, types of credit, and number of credit inquiries. FICO scores range from 300 to 850, with higher scores signifying stronger creditworthiness.

[7] While a FICO score of 660 was highlighted as the minimum threshold by Fannie and Freddie, a score of 620 or below was considered too low to meet GSE standards. Ed Pinto focuses on the 660 score to show the transition of the GSEs into riskier lending.

CHAPTER 3: *Race to the Bottom*

[1] See Jack Favilukis, Sydney Ludvigson, and Stijn Van Nieuwerburgh, "The Macroeconomic Effects of Housing Wealth, Housing Finance, and Limited Risk-Sharing in General Equilibrium," Working Paper, New York University Stern School of Business, 2010, for a formal model of this credit expansion and the associated house price appreciation.

[2] Alt-A is a short name for alternative-to-agency (such as those of the GSEs) mortgages. An Alt-A mortgage is a type of U.S. mortgage that is considered riskier than prime mortgages and less risky than subprime, the riskiest category. Typically Alt-A mortgages are characterized by borrowers with less than full documentation, lower credit scores, higher loan-to-value ratios, and more investment properties. A-minus is related to Alt-A, with some lenders categorizing them the same way, but A-minus is traditionally defined as mortgage borrowers with a FICO credit score of below 680 whereas Alt-A is traditionally defined as loans that lack full documentation. Alt-A mortgages may have excellent credit but may not meet underwriting criteria for other reasons.

[3] This point of a regulatory race to the bottom is not new to the economic theory of the political economy of regulation. If a set of institutions (Fannie and Freddie) enjoys stronger guarantees but lower capital requirements, then other institutions (investment banks) with access to weaker guarantees employ lobbying for similar treatment. In turn, the regulator of these other institutions, if sufficiently captured (even if just cognitively so), would adopt lower capital requirements also. If anything, this theory would suggest that the first set of institutions that enjoy stronger guarantees should be subject to *higher* capital requirements to avoid the "regulatory race to the bottom." See Viral V. Acharya, "Is the International Convergence of Capital Adequacy

Regulation Desirable?" *Journal of Finance* 58 (6, December 2003): 2745–81.

[4] Viral V. Acharya, Thomas Cooley, Matthew Richardson, and Ingo Walter, "Manufacturing Tail Risk: A Perspective on the Financial Crisis of 2007–09," *Foundations and Trends in Finance* 4 (4, 2010): 247–325, argue that the manufacturing of tail risk on certain mortgage-backed securities was a central feature of the financial crisis.

[5] These off-balance-sheet vehicles were funded with 100% leverage on their own, holding long-maturity mortgage and corporate loan assets, but funded overnight by asset-backed commercial paper (ABCP)—a form of wholesale finance mainly from money market funds. This form of off-balance-sheet leverage grew in size from $600 billion to more than $1,200 billion in just three years, from 2004 to 2007. See Viral V. Acharya, Philipp Schnabl, and Gustavo Suarez, "Securitization without Risk Transfer," Working Paper, New York University Stern School of Business, 2009.

[6] In a historical account of crises over eight centuries, Carmen Reinhart and Kenneth Rogoff, *This Time Is Different: Eight Centuries of Financial Folly* (Princeton: Princeton University Press, 2010), discuss the role played by capital inflows in engendering a vast number of financial crises. Raghuram Rajan, *Fault Lines: How Hidden Fractures Still Threaten the World Economy* (Princeton: Princeton University Press, 2010), also attributes the crisis of 2007–9 to the global imbalances that have resulted in substantial flows from surplus countries (such as China) to deficit countries (such as the United States and the United Kingdom) and provided "easy money" for governments of deficit countries and their financial sectors to misallocate credit.

[7] These results are generally consistent with those presented by Dwight Jaffee, in April 2010, in testimony before the Financial

Crisis Inquiry Commission that the GSEs engaged in large dollar volumes of high-risk lending in each of the years 2003 to 2007. See table 3.3 in Dwight M. Jaffee, "The Role of the GSEs and Housing Policy in the Financial Crisis," Testimony for the Financial Crisis Inquiry Commission, February 27, 2010, Washington, DC.

CHAPTER 4: *Too Big to Fail*

1 See Treasury Under Secretary Gary Gensler's speech to the House Banking Subcommittee on Capital Markets, Securities and Government Sponsored Enterprises, March 22, 2000, available at http://www.ustreas.gov/press/releases/ls479.htm.

2 Source: Lehman Brothers, "Residential Credit Losses—Going into Extra Innings?" April 11, 2008.

3 See Viral V. Acharya, Philipp Schnabl, and Gustavo Suarez, "Securitization without Risk Transfer," Working Paper, New York University Stern School of Business, 2009.

4 There is also an entirely over-the-counter and bilateral repo market that tends to be between large dealers and hedge funds and is often for more illiquid and riskier collateral than Treasuries and Agencies. Adam Copeland, Antoine Martin, and Michael Walker, "The Tri-Party Repo Market before the 2010 Reforms," Working Paper, Federal Reserve Bank of New York, 2010, explain the important differences in operations and during-crisis behavior between the triparty repo market and the dealer-hedge fund repo market.

5 Viral V. Acharya and T. Sabri Oncu, "The Repurchase Agreement (Repo) Market," chapter 11 in *Regulating Wall Street: The*

Dodd-Frank Act and the New Architecture of Global Finance, edited by Viral V. Acharya, Thomas Cooley, Matthew Richardson, and Ingo Walter (Hoboken, NJ: John Wiley & Sons, 2010).

[6] CBO report, "Assessing the Public Costs and Benefits of Fannie Mae and Freddie Mac," May 1996, p. 44.

[7] Patrick Hosking, Christine Seib, Marcus Leroux, and Grainne Gilmore, "Run on the Bank," *Sunday Times*, September 15, 2007.

[8] Henry M. Paulson Jr., *On the Brink: Inside the Race to Stop the Collapse of the Global Financial System* (New York: Business Plus, 2010), p. 159.

CHAPTER 5: *End of Days*

[1] http://www.huduser.org/publications/pdf/CMAR_VegasNV.pdf.

[2] "CBO's Budgetary Treatment of Fannie Mae and Freddie Mac," Congressional Budget Office Background Paper, January 2010. According to its August 2010 projection, the CBO estimates that mortgage guarantees and portfolio investments by Fannie Mae and Freddie Mac will add $53 billion to the budget for the 2011–20 period.

[3] The day-to-day management of the mortgage is left to a servicer, who typically is in closest contact with the borrower and who collects a fee that is based on the size of the loan. The servicer must decide whether to modify each mortgage. This arrangement has led some to worry that servicers either lack the authority or have insufficient incentives to undertake costly modifications.

[4] Tomasz Piskorski, Amit Seru, and Vikrant Vig, "Securitization and Distressed Loan Renegotiation: Evidence from the Subprime Mortgage Crisis," Research Paper No. 09-02, Chicago Booth School of Business, August 2009.

[5] John P. Hunt, "What Do Subprime Securitization Contracts Actually Say about Loan Modification?" Berkeley Center for Law, Business, and the Economy Working Paper, March 2009.

[6] Andrew Haughwout, Ebiere Okah, and Joseph S. Tracy, "Second Chances: Subprime Mortgage Modification and Re-Default," Federal Reserve Bank of New York Working Paper, 2009.

[7] See Viral V. Acharya, Philipp Schnabl, and Gustavo Suarez, "Securitization without Risk Transfer," Working Paper, New York University Stern School of Business, 2009.

[8] See Adam Ashcraft, Morten Beck, and W. Scott Frame, "The Federal Home Loan Bank System: The Lender of Next-to-Last Resort?" Working Paper, Federal Reserve Bank of New York, 2009.

[9] Ibid.

CHAPTER 6: *In Bed with the Fed*

[1] For a succinct history of central banking in the United States, see Thomas Cooley, Kermit Schoenholtz, George Smith, Richard Sylla, and Paul Wachtel, "The Power of Central Banks and the Future of the Federal Reserve System," chapter 2 in *Regulating Wall Street: The Dodd-Frank Act and the New Architecture of Global Finance*, edited by Viral V. Acharya, Thomas Cooley, Matthew

Richardson, and Ingo Walter (Hoboken, NJ: John Wiley & Sons, 2010).

[2] In his diary from days when the conservatorship plan was being hatched in July 2008, the then treasury secretary Henry Paulson recounts that the Federal Reserve governor Ben Bernanke recognized that this was clearly a fiscal matter but that the Board of Governors would consider it in the interest of financial stability if the Treasury were to be granted emergency authorities to take over the GSEs and avoid a disorderly liquidation by markets. Henry M. Paulson Jr., *On the Brink: Inside the Race to Stop the Collapse of the Global Financial System* (New York: Business Plus, 2010).

[3] The authors are grateful to Kim Schoenholtz for useful discussions regarding this point. See also David H. Small and James A. Clouse, "The Scope of Monetary Policy Actions Authorized under the Federal Reserve Act," Working Paper, Board of Governors of the Federal Reserve, 2004, for understanding the ways and extent to which the Federal Reserve Act limits (and does not limit) the Fed from taking credit risk onto its balance sheet.

[4] Chairman of the Board of Governors of the Federal Reserve, Ben Bernanke, called this the "portfolio balance channel" and attributed success to the Fed's quantitative easing program to altering the mix of investors' portfolio mix ("The Economic Outlook and Monetary Policy," Remarks at the Federal Reserve Bank of Kansas City Economic Symposium at Jackson Hole, Wyoming, August 27, 2010).

[5] See Zhiguo He, In Gu Khang, and Arvind Krishnamurthy, "Balance Sheet Adjustments in the 2008 Crisis," *IMF Economic Review* 58 (1, 2010): 118–56. It details how the overall adjustment of the financial sector's balance sheet took place as far as mortgage-backed securities were concerned between commercial

banks, investment banks, hedge funds, insurance firms, the GSEs, and the Federal Reserve.

[6] Narayana Kocherlakota, "Economic Outlook and Economic Choices," Speech by the President of the Federal Reserve Bank of Minneapolis, May 13, 2010.

[7] For a more complete description of how the Dodd-Frank Act of 2010 limits the scope of the Federal Reserve's emergency lending facilities, see Cooley et al., "The Power of Central Banks and the Future of the Federal Reserve System" (see note 1).

[8] Eric Leeper calls this situation an "era of fiscal stress" and highlights the risk that it may be especially likely when governments do not have a well-stated (or well-understood) fiscal policy, as in the case of United States, for example, with respect to dealing with its huge, currently off-balance-sheet entitlements to health care and pensions. ("Monetary Science, Fiscal Alchemy," presentation at the Federal Reserve Bank of Kansas City Economic Symposium at Jackson Hole, Wyoming, August 28, 2010).

[9] Testimony to the House Financial Services Committee, February 10, 2010.

CHAPTER 7: *How Others Do It*

[1] Examples include recent work by Gary Gorton and Andrew Metrick, who argue that securitization is a rework on traditional banking and has not developed to transfer the credit risk away from banks, while work by the NYU Stern School of Business on the crisis describes securitization as an important tool for banks to exploit loopholes in capital requirements: regulatory arbitrage. Gary B. Gorton and Andrew Metric, "Securitized Banking and

the Run on Repo," Working Paper no. 09-14, Yale University, and Viral V. Acharya and Matthew Richardson, eds., *Restoring Financial Stability: How to Repair a Failed System* (Hoboken, NJ: Wiley, 2009).

[2] For an explanation of the fluctuations in the share of fixed-rate mortgages in the United States over time, see Ralph Koijen, Otto Van Hemert, and Stijn Van Nieuwerburgh, "Mortgage Timing," *Journal of Financial Economics* 93 (2, 2009): 292–324.

[3] These states are Alaska, Arizona, California, Connecticut, Florida, Idaho, Minnesota, North Carolina, North Dakota, Texas, Utah, and Washington. In some states such as California, home equity lines of credit and home equity loans are recourse loans, even though original home loans are non-recourse.

[4] One of the important factors that explain why banking balance sheets in some countries became excessively leveraged was the ease with which commercial banks could set up off-balance-sheet vehicles and exploit loopholes in Basel capital requirements to reduce their regulatory capital requirements. See Viral V. Acharya and Philipp Schnabl, "Do Global Banks Spread Global Imbalances? Asset-Backed Commercial Paper in the Financial Crisis of 2007–09," *IMF Economic Review* 58 (1, 2010): 37–73.

CHAPTER 8: *How to Reform a Broken System*

[1] Nadezhda Malysheva and John R. Walter, "How Large Has the Federal Financial Safety Net Become?" Federal Reserve Bank of Richmond, Working Paper, March 2010.

[2] Former Federal Reserve governor Alan Greenspan attributes the liquidity of mortgage markets to securitization rather than

the extent of GSE portfolio holdings of mortgages. In a speech to the Conference on Housing, Mortgage Finance, and the Macroeconomy, Federal Reserve Bank of Atlanta, Atlanta, Georgia, dedicated to the theme of government-sponsored enterprises (http://www.federalreserve.gov/boarddocs/speeches/2005/20050519/), he noted: "Since the development of the MBS market, the determinants of interest rates that finance home purchase have exhibited little, if any, response to the size of GSE portfolios."

[3] Edward S. Prescott,. "Can Risk-Based Deposit Insurance Premiums Control Moral Hazard?" Federal Reserve Bank of Richmond *Economic Quarterly*, Spring 2002, pp. 87–100.

[4] See Viral V. Acharya, Barry Adler, Nouriel Roubini, and Matthew Richardson, "Resolution Authority," chapter 8 in *Regulating Wall Street: The Dodd-Frank Act and the New Architecture of Global Finance,* edited by Viral V. Acharya, Thomas Cooley, Matthew Richardson, and Ingo Walter (Hoboken, NJ: John Wiley & Sons, 2010).

[5] Note that this feature closely resembles that of covered bonds, which is one of the more popular mortgage finance instruments that are employed internationally, as is described in chapter 7.

[6] MBA Response to the Administration's Questions on the Secondary Market and GSEs, June 17, 2010.

[7] Toni Dechario, Patricia Mosser, Joseph Tracy, James Vickery, and Joshua Wright, "A Private Lender Cooperative Model for Residential Mortgage Finance," Federal Reserve Bank of New York, Staff Report no. 466, August 2010.

[8] Numbers based on First American Core logic's report on the number of homeowners who are underwater on their mortgages,

and Deutsche Bank's Securitization Reports on distribution of home equity in the housing market.

[9] This is not to say that there would be no government involvement in nonconforming mortgages. Chapter 9 describes the current FHA and VA model for supporting affordable housing, and we would expect that to continue in some form, whether it be home ownership or renting. To prevent a GSE-like entity from emerging, however, the program should be limited in scope and, to ensure this, should define low mortgage limits and reduce the program to primary homes.

[10] Viral V. Acharya, Lasse Pedersen, Thomas Philippon, and Matthew Richardson, "Taxing Systemic Risk," chapter 5 in *Regulating Wall Street: The Dodd-Frank Act and the New Architecture of Global Finance,* edited by Viral V. Acharya, Thomas Cooley, Matthew Richardson, and Ingo Walter (Hoboken, NJ: John Wiley & Sons, 2010).

[11] The "shadow banking system" describes the parallel method of financing loans that developed wholly outside the traditional depository (banks and thrifts) system during the past few decades, especially for mortgages. The mortgages can be originated by mortgage companies, sold to securities packagers (including investment banks and the GSEs), who then sell the mortgage-backed securities (containing pools of mortgages) to investors (such as pension funds, insurance companies, mutual funds, and hedge funds).

[12] John Geanakoplos. "Solving the Present Crisis and Managing the Leverage Cycle," *Federal Reserve Bank of New York Economic Policy Review*, August 2010, pp. 101–31.

[13] This is feasible to the extent that before the start of the crisis, there was a liquid market for residential and commercial MBS

indices, called ABX and CMBX. These indices are constructed from a representative basket of MBS of a given vintage, with two vintages per year. The idea for these indices came from the CDS market, where baskets of single-name CDSs were traded in the form of a CDX index.

[14] HR 4173, Title I, "Financial Stability," Subtitle A, "Financial Stability Oversight Council," Sec. 115, "Enhanced Supervision and Prudential Standards for Nonbank Financial Companies Supervised by the Board of Governors and Certain Bank Holding Companies."

[15] "Basel" is shorthand for the set of international agreements on the prudential regulation of banks that have been developed since the 1980s under the auspices of the Bank for International Settlements (BIS), which is located in Basel.

[16] HR 4173, Title II, "Orderly Liquidation Authority," Sec. 204, "Orderly Liquidation of Covered Financial Companies."

[17] HR 4173, Title IX, subtitle D, Sec. 941, "Credit Risk Retention."

[18] HR 4173, Title XIV, subtitle B, "Minimum Standards for Mortgages."

CHAPTER 9: *Chasing the Dragon*

[1] Other actions by the U.S. government throughout the financial crisis to deal with the mortgage market include, among others, a change in the conforming loan limit from $417,000 to a maximum $729,750 (depending on the location), liquidity facilities at the Fed accepting mortgage-backed securities (MBS) collateral, purchases of MBS and government-sponsored enterprise (GSE)

debt by the Fed and Treasury, and Home Affordable Modification Programs by the GSEs.

[2] Edwin S. Mills, "Has the United States Overinvested in Housing?" *Journal of the American Real Estate and Urban Economics Association* 15 (Spring 1987): 601–16; and Edwin S. Mills, "Dividing up the Investment Pie: Have We Overinvested in Housing?" Federal Reserve Bank of Philadelphia *Business Review,* March–April 1987, pp. 13–23.

[3] According to the National Homeownership Strategy document of 1995, home ownership promotes commitment to family, good citizenship, and community and gives people greater control and responsibility over their environment and greater incentive to improve and maintain private property and public spaces. It promotes personal financial security through the accumulation of home equity.

[4] Home ownership has benefits both for the individual and for society. A 2001 Harvard University Joint Center for Housing Studies Working Paper by William M. Rohe, Shannon Van Zandt, and George McCarthy, titled "The Social Benefits and Costs of Homeownership: A Critical Assessment of the Research" studies individual social impacts on satisfaction, psychological health, and physical health and societal social impacts on neighborhood stability, social involvement, and socially desirable youth behaviors. The authors conclude that the evidence suggests, for example, that homeowners are more likely to be satisfied with their homes and neighborhoods, more likely to participate in voluntary and political activities, and more likely to stay in their homes longer periods of time. Some doubt still exists, however, whether these relationships are causal, because most of the studies do not adequately account for the self-selection of households to owner and renter occupancy. Evidence of the impacts of home ownership on other social variables is more sparse and

less consistent. The research on the impacts of home ownership on both perceived control and socially desirable youth behaviors is simply too sparse to draw conclusions. More troubling, very little research exists on potential negative social impacts of home ownership, for example, the effect of foreclosures on psychological and physical health and on neighborhood stability. Finally, the consensus view is that home ownership leads to less mobility, especially in times when many households have negative equity, making labor markets less efficient.

[5] Karsten Jeske, Dirk Krueger, and Kurt Mitman, "Housing and the Macroeconomy: The Role of Implicit Guarantees for Government Sponsored Enterprises," University of Pennsylvania Working Paper, February 2010.

[6] Gervais, Martin, "Housing Taxation and Capital Accumulation," *Journal of Monetary Economics* 49 (7, 2001): 1461–89.

[7] James Poterba and Todd Sinai, "Tax Expenditures for Owner-Occupied Housing: Deductions for Property Taxes and Mortgage Interest and the Exclusion of Imputed Rental Income," National Bureau of Economic Research Working Paper, 2008.

[8] Even this, however, is heavily debated. As Alan Greenspan notes in a speech to the Conference on Housing, Mortgage Finance, and the Macroeconomy, Federal Reserve Bank of Atlanta, Atlanta, Georgia, dedicated to the theme of government-sponsored enterprises (http://www.federalreserve.gov/boarddocs/speeches/2005/20050519/): "Some observers have suggested that the availability of fixed-rate mortgages is tied to the size of GSE portfolios. We see little empirical support for this notion. For example, we have found no evidence that fixed-rate mortgages were difficult to obtain during the early 1990s, when GSE portfolios were small. Indeed, the share of fixed-rate mortgage originations averaged slightly less than 80 percent in 1992, when GSE portfolios were

small, and averaged 66 percent in 2004, when GSE portfolios were large. Clearly, these data do not support the proposition that the size of the GSEs' portfolios positively contributes to the availability or popularity of fixed-rate mortgages. It is, of course, mortgage securitization, and not GSE portfolios, that is the more likely reason for the continued market support for the popular thirty-year fixed-rate mortgage."

[9] Raphael Bostic and Stuart Gabriel analyzed census tract averages of GSE purchase activity and housing outcomes for census tracts with median incomes at the boundaries of those specified in the GSE housing goals and those specified in the 1977 Community Reinvestment Act. An intensive analysis of California census tracts found a positive association between GSE activity and housing market conditions, home ownership rates, and vacancies, but the association is generally not statistically meaningful. Raphael W. Bostic, and Stuart A. Gabriel, "Do the GSEs Matter to Low-Income Housing Markets? An Assessment of the Effects of the GSE Loan Purchase Goals on California Housing Outcomes," *Journal of Urban Economics* 59 (3, 2006): 458–75.

[10] Jack Favilukis, Sydney Ludvigson, and Stijn Van Nieuwerburgh, "The Macroeconomic Effects of Housing Wealth, Housing Finance, and Limited Risk Sharing in General Equilibrium," Working Paper, New York University, 2010; and Edward L. Glaeser, with Joshua Gottlieb and Joseph Gyourko, "Can Cheap Credit Explain the Housing Boom?" Working Paper, Harvard University, 2010.

Epilogue

[1] The analogy of fighting oil fires with respect to the financial crisis derives from comments made by Nobel Prize–winning

economist Myron Scholes at an NYU Stern School of Business conference in March 2009 for the school's launch of its first book on the crisis, *Restoring Financial Stability: How to Repair a Failed System*. The Red Adair–Fred Astaire comment is taken from an exchange between Myron Scholes and John Gapper, the *Financial Time*'s chief business commentator at that time.

AFTERWORD: GOVERNMENT-SPONSORED ENTERPRISES AND INDIA

"Jyan Raja Vyapari, Tyan Praja Bhikhari"
(Where King is a Trader, Subjects are Beggars)

—Gujarati proverb

To an Indian, it might seem surprising that a book on government-sponsored enterprises (GSEs) should be written with the backdrop of housing finance in the United States. Government involvement – or interference – in the economy and financial markets, of the sort displayed by Fannie Mae and Freddie Mac, has traditionally been the prerogative of governments in less developed economies with full or partial control over the financial sector, rather than in the bastion of capitalism, the United States. Yet, the beauty of an economist's lens is that the more it sees the world, the more it looks the same: that where there are government-sponsored enterprises, there are government-sponsored crises.

So what are the similarities between the United States and India as far as government involvement in finance is concerned?

Are there lingering risks for India of the form that were manifested for the United States through the risk-taking and eventual collapse of Fannie and Freddie? What preventive – or corrective – measures can India undertake in order to avoid a government-sponsored crisis? Or is India, the democracy with the greatest growth potential over the next few decades, destined to run into similar problems as the United States, its democratic counterpart of the last century?

First and foremost, it is important to recognize that India is a tale of two parallel economies, not the white-money and the black-money economies that immediately comes to mind, but of fast-paced urban India and sluggish rural India. Urban India provides most of the significant manufacturing and services growth to the economy, has affluent families even if co-existing with highly poor ones, and exhibits reasonable levels of access to bank savings, stock markets, mutual funds, insurance products, and the like. Rural India, in contrast, is farming-focused, is relatively poor with current earning that is less than $2 per day, and has abysmal levels of financial inclusion. As per statistics from the International Institute for Strategic Studies (IISS, 2007), only 14 percent of agricultural wage laborers had a bank account, whereas the number was over 85 percent for self-employed professionals. While agricultural wage labor does have access to informal savings schemes, that is a second-best solution (in the economic parlance) rather than the first-best. Given such a lack of financial inclusion in rural India, which comprises over 75 percent of India's population by most estimates, there is both an economic and a political case for improving access to finance. How can the government achieve the transition for rural India, in terms of growth and financial access, to levels that are at least comparable to those of urban India, if not of the most developed economies?

Unfortunately, answers in India to questions of this sort have by and large been of brute-force interventions, rather than a nuanced enabling of the private sector in aiding such a transition. The experiment of Fabian Socialism sapped the private sector of its growth potential for close to four decades post-independence, and continued to leave an indelible imprint even through the reforms of the 1990s. Political forces ensured that a series of successive governments, under one pretext or the other, preserved the government hegemony over a large number of business segments (oil, natural gas, power, aviation, among others) that are yet to be privatized or are at best poorly privatized. While this imprint in itself would call for a separate treatment, more relevant to this book would be looking at the government efforts to improve financial inclusion.

This is where the Indian government-sponsored enterprises in the financial sector come into play. Currently, the Indian banking sector is partly state-owned. State-owned banks own over 70 percent of banking assets; until the 1990s' reforms, the state ownership of the banking sector was in fact 100 percent. Indeed, India is one of the nine countries in the world to have a predominantly state-owned banking sector (the others being Bhutan, Libya, Algeria, Belarus, Turkmenistan, Egypt and Costa Rica). Among fast-growing emerging markets, its state presence in banking is paralleled only by China. State-owned banks in India enjoy privileged branching, especially in rural areas, where the private sector, often eager to enter, is by and large restricted from entry, or at least not allowed to enter by default.

The origins of such desire for state control of rural finance are many. It is partly rooted in the socialist view of the economy that took immediate hold following independence, but it is largely a matter of political convenience. It is important to keep over 75 percent of India's population happy, at least in the short term, when they are about to cast important votes. Not surprisingly, a telling study by Shawn Cole of the Harvard Business School, published in the *American Economic Journal* (*Applied Economics*, 2009), and aptly titled "Fixing Market Failures or Fixing Elections?", found that agricultural lending in India has a cyclical pattern that is not coincident with the economic cycle of the country but with the political cycle.

There are distinct parallels between this foray of the Indian government into rural banking and the role of Fannie Mae and Freddie Mac in the United States. First, affordable home ownership goals of the United States relate to "priority sector lending norms" in India (focused on agriculture and small-scale industries, but also include housing). Second, the GSEs in the United States correspond to the large presence of state-owned banks in India. Third, the forbearance that was exhibited towards the GSEs – in good times through generous capital requirements and in bad times through government conservatism – mirrors closely the reluctance of the Indian government to shut down any state-owned bank (or rural cooperatives that also aid the priority sector lending goals). Fourth, as over time, the GSEs in the US crowded out the private financial sector in affordable housing loans, so have the state-owned banks in India. The annual income of bank customers in private and foreign banks in India are substantially greater than those of the customers of public-sector and cooperative banks; and yet, like the quality of sub-prime loans of GSEs, the non-performing assets from priority sector loans are greater for state-owned Indian banks than for private and foreign banks in India.

The Indian state has thus freely traded in credit extension to the poor in a manner that is similar to that of the United States government. Alas, it too has condemned its poor to be even poorer in the process. A bulk of the priority sector lending in India goes to farming loans. Since banks are effectively forced to lend at quantities that they would not lend at had they been entirely private and free of state-enforced lending norms, the quality of the lending is poor. Put simply, lending happens down the quality curve up to a point that is not worthy of finance. In turn, even low-productivity farming and agricultural investment in rural India can be readily financed. Of course, loans in such investments go bad, but most of the losses are concentrated in state-owned and cooperative banks. The strong clutch of the government now becomes a crutch, readily extending support where the invisible hand of the market would have resulted in shutting down of banks. Since these banks never fail, they do not care about the quality of their loans. Since they do not exercise due diligence with respect to borrowers, the farmers do not invest in highly productive and innovative agricultural methods. And of course, they do not consider retooling to any other skill set besides farming. Thus, neither the banks nor the farmers are subject to the capitalist creative destruction that would seem essential for success in a country where the rural, farming-focused, sector is so large, yet low on productivity.

One wonders, in fact, if the demographic dividends that India is supposed to reap in the next few decades – by virtue of an anticipated decline in its dependent to working-age population ratio – will be more than offset by the negative dividends resulting from the poor quality of farming. In a country of over 1.21 billion people by the latest census, with a rapidly expanding middle-class, investments in productive farming ought to find center stage. Yet, India stumbles from year to year, facing acute food shortages that fluctuate with the vicissitudes of tropical monsoons and create a never-ending predicament for the Reserve Bank of India (RBI), India's central bank, as to whether to fight food inflation through interest-rate hikes or aid the economy's reaping of its demographic dividends through interest-rate cuts. As the RBI's deputy governor, Dr Subir Gokarn, commented in his piece in the *Financial Times* on 29 March, 2011, "Food inflation, covering both unprocessed and processed items, already at a relatively high 10.4 percent in June 2009 (when the headline rate troughed) soared to 20.2 percent in December 2009. It has come down since then, but has remained high at 6.4 percent in February 2011 … All along, the objective was to not disrupt the growth recovery, while containing the spread of inflationary pressures from food and energy into a wider process. The Reserve Bank, therefore, chose a steady, calibrated response. Given the significance of supply side inflationary pressures throughout the period, stronger interest rate actions might have slowed growth far more than they would have slowed inflation."

Let us turn now to another recurring theme of our treatment of how Fannie Mae and Freddie Mac eventually failed. This was the "race to the bottom" between the public sector and the private sector in the United States finance. Paradoxically, the mother of all failures – those of Fannie and Freddie – ended up with these entities owning the mother of all shares in the mortgage finance post-crisis in the United States. Something similar, albeit on a smaller scale, happened in India in 2008 as well, when the genie of government guarantees surreptitiously crept up, stabilizing the banking sector but eroding the private banks. The genie needs to be put back in the bottle now, but government guarantees are unfortunately being anointed as the pillar of modern Indian banking.

Let us rewind to 2008. The crisis hit India somewhat unexpectedly. In early 2008, there were talks of how "decoupled" emerging markets such as India and China had become from the financial and economic malaise of the Western economies. However, the interconnected nature of the global financial plumbing debunked any such myth rather quickly. In the case of India, a number of large multinational firms had external bank and corporate bond borrowings in foreign currencies and markets. As the Western financial sector started unraveling in early September of 2008 and Lehman Brothers filed for bankruptcy on September 15, the market freezes abroad created a severe liquidity shortage for these Indian firms. Their immediate response was to ask for redemption of their savings from the Indian money-market funds. As these funds faced liquidations of their portfolio holdings, they also withdrew from their lending to financial institutions, including banks. The precautionary measure by Indian corporations, stemming from the market freeze abroad, effectively began to translate into a freeze in the Indian inter-bank markets. While all this was happening, the stock market had already witnessed a 50 percent drop from its peak at the end of 2007, and some private-sector Indian banks with foreign exposures were under watch by investors for a potential run. What ensued was in many ways magical in the short run, but entrenched the stronghold of public-sector banking in India even further.

Savers in the Indian economy, fearing a banking crisis and runs on the private-sector banks, started moving their deposits to public-sector banks. As per Reserve Bank of India estimates, public sector bank deposits grew by 24.1 percent during fiscal year 2009 (March 2008–March 2009) compared to a 22.9 percent growth a year earlier. In comparison, private-sector deposit growth slowed from 19.9 percent to a mere 8 percent for the same periods. In anecdotal evidence that is consistent with this "flight-to-government-guarantee", Infosys transferred nearly Rs 10 billion of deposits from ICICI Bank (a private-sector bank) to the State Bank of India (the largest public-sector bank) just after Lehman's collapse. And unsurprisingly, when the Indian government announced a number of wide-ranging stimulus plans to jumpstart the ailing banking system, several weak public-sector banks received a significant share of stimulus to restore their capital levels.

The flight of deposits in this episode appears to have stacked the odds against the private financial sector considerably since. They are, in effect, getting somewhat crowded out. The credit for public sector banks grew by 20.4 percent in 2009 compared to 22.5 percent in 2008, whereas for private sector banks, it grew by only 10.9 percent compared to 19.9 percent in 2008. In the retail segment, public-sector banks came out with inexpensive housing, auto, and education loans, emerging as the lead financers in the Tata Nano auto purchases. The ruling party claimed that "public sector financial institutions have given our economy the stability and resilience we are now witnessing in the face of the economic slowdown." And while such stability and resilience has converted – perhaps just reinforced – Indian public-sector banks into the equivalent of GSE Godzillas, the private-sector King Kongs have recently complained, as they did in the United States about Fannie and Freddie's low-cost funding, that public-sector bank schemes are primarily undercutting competitors given the former's implicitly guaranteed funding base.

All evidence suggests that the state-banking sector in India grew during the crisis at the expense of private banks, as also formally confirmed in a recent academic study by Viral Acharya (one of the authors of this book) and Nirupama Kulkarni of Haas School of Business at the University of Berkeley in their piece titled, "State Ownership and Systemic Risk: Evidence from the Indian Financial Sector during 2007–09". The government, however, is yet to recognize – or acknowledge – that the growth of state-owned banking sector since 2008 has been the effect of state guarantees, *not* state ownership. Banks all over the world were stabilized – whether public or private – once governments back-stopped them. This emergency back-stop, the emergence of the genie out of the bottle, need not however be coincident with the misfortunes associated with state ownership in good times. One, state ownership creates the severe moral hazard of directing bank lending for politically expedient goals and of bailouts when such lending goes bad. Second, it restricts the ability of state-owned banks from raising arm's length capital against state's stake, strangling their growth and keeping these banks – and certainly their private capital base – smaller than it need be.

Until recently, there was a consistent trend towards the privatization of the banking sector in India. However, the recent underperformance by private sector banks has raised some doubts regarding this approach and created a political consensus against the pre-crisis notion that state-owned banks be fully privatized in due course. Many see this as another nail in the coffin of efficient privatization of sectors that have a significant presence of the Indian state. Our story has been that government-sponsored enterprises morph into hedge funds of the likes of Fannie and

Freddie that are *guaranteed to fail*. This should strike a note of caution to the stance of Indian policymakers against drawing conclusions favoring state presence in the financial sector.

Indeed, an Indian GSE has been before where Fannie and Freddie are now. The free trade by the Indian state historically extended beyond credit markets. In 1963, the Indian state created the Unit Trust of India (UTI), which for more than two decades remained the sole vehicle for investment in the capital market by Indian citizens. In the mid-1980s, public sector banks were allowed to open mutual funds. The UTI rode the stock-market rise of the 1990s till the "Ketan Parekh scam" burst the bubble. UTI's flagship and largest scheme, US 64, had promised returns as high as 18 percent over a period going up to two decades. A full-fledged run on the Indian stock markets would have likely ensued had the government not come out with a rescue package. The UTI Act was repealed, the UTI broken up; UTI Mutual Fund still runs now, but like any other mutual fund, controlling less than 10 percent share of the market and operating at a distance from the government. UTI, like Fannie and Freddie, was just that – guaranteed to fail – a government-sponsored hedge fund that brought about a government-sponsored crisis.

And while it has not led to a significant crisis so far, the Life Insurance Corporation (LIC) of India, the largest state-owned life insurance company, is again also the country's largest investor. The penetration of its insurance business in rural India, which might seem to be the primary goal of the state owning such an enterprise, is far less impressive than its penetration as an investor, funding close to 25 percent of the Indian government's expenses, most notably through public-sector projects like dams.

Government guarantees – explicit or implicit – and investor anticipation of a safety net for public sector banks and similar vehicles have deep consequences for competitive forces in the financial sector, potentially shaping their long-run form, and always stacking the odds against the flourishing of private players. How will the private-sector banks in India respond to the emerging strength of public-sector banks? Will they undertake greater risks and leverage in order to compensate for their likely underperformance when the next crisis hits? Can India afford such a race to the bottom when over 70 percent of the banking assets are funded in a manner that effectively represents off balance-sheet liabilities of the government? And this too, in times when India's fiscal deficit as a percentage of its GDP is among the highest in the world? Similarly, will the private insurance sector be able to grow with reasonable premiums for a deprived population from a starting point where it must compete with LIC's effective monopoly and national champion status? As the UTI's "unwinding" shows, things work out well in the private sector when the government lets go off its muscular grip.

While the macro-prudential policies of the Reserve Bank of India have stood India in good stead against the real-estate boom and inflation risks to date, they are likely to come under increasing strain if the private financial sector sees demographic dividends disappearing beyond a few years and feels the heat to compete aggressively with the public players. Will the RBI's asset-level leverage restrictions such as loan-to-value (LTV) ratios be meaningful if banks are lending at sub-par rates and housing prices – denominators in the LTV ratios – are heavily inflated? Would non-bank financial firms develop a world of "shadow banking" for the private financial sector to park risks away from the scrutiny of the RBI? Would it not be better instead to create a level playing field where all financial firms are private, but are charged upfront for government guarantees in the form of deposit insurance (up to reasonable ceilings), allowed to branch freely in rural areas as growth demands, and subject to a clear resolution authority, so that both financial firms and their borrowers undergo creative destruction and are thus incentivized to innovate and experiment? With better-run banks and a faster-growing economy, the economy could be weaned off priority-sector norms in due course down to a *de minimis* level.

India was a darling of the Western media in 2010. Its demographic appeal and democratic politics make it a country whose growth much of the world would like to see flourish in the decades to come. Yet, we worry that India's Achilles' heel may well be the same as that of the United States: an overarching clutch of the government rather than the gentle invisible arm of private financial markets; a distortive government-directed lending practice in the financial sector rather than just a nuanced macro-prudential policy operated by the central bank; an excessively large but inefficient farming sector with inflated food prices comparable to the housing sector of the United States; and, in the end, the lack of a political will in the state to stop being the king-trader and uplift its millions of subjects from poverty.

GLOSSARY

ABCP: asset-backed commercial paper
ABS: asset-backed securities
AIG: American International Group
Alt-A: alternative to agency (mortgage)
ARM: adjustable-rate mortgage
BIS: Bank for International Settlements
BNY: Bank of New York Mellon
CBO: Congressional Budget Office
CDO: collateralized debt obligation
CDS: credit default swap
CEO: chief executive officer
CFPB: Consumer Finance Protection Bureau
CLTV: combined loan-to-value ratio
CMO: collateralized mortgage obligation
DTI: debt-to-income ratio
FDIC: Federal Deposit Insurance Corporation
FHA: Federal Housing Administration
FHEFSSA : Federal Housing Enterprises Financial Safety and Soundness Act
FHFA: Federal Housing Finance Agency
FHLB: Federal Home Loan Banks
FHLMC: Federal Home Loan Mortgage Corporation, a.k.a. Freddie Mac
FICO: Fair-Isaac Corporation (credit score)

FIRREA: Financial Institutions Reform, Recovery, and Enforcement Act
FNMA: Federal National Mortgage Association, a.k.a. Fannie Mae
FRA: Federal Reserve Act
FRM: fixed-rate mortgage
FSLIC: Federal Savings and Loan Insurance Corporation
GDP: gross domestic product
GMRIC: Government Mortgage Risk Insurance Corporation
GNMA: Government National Mortgage Association, a.k.a. Ginnie Mae
GSE: government-sponsored enterprise
HAMP: Home Affordable Modification Program
HELOC: home equity line of credit
HERA: Housing and Economic Recovery Act
HOLA: Home Owners Loan Act
HUD: Department of Housing and Urban Development

IMF: International Monetary Fund
LC: letter of credit
LCFI: large complex financial institution
LOLR: lender of last resort
LTCM: Long-Term Capital Management
LTV: loan-to-value ratio; see also CLTV
MBA: Mortgage Bankers Association
MBS: mortgage-backed securities
MCGE: mortgage credit guarantor entity
NAMA: National Asset Management Agency (Ireland)
NHA: National Housing Act
NINJA: no income, no job, and no assets (mortgage)
NY Fed: Federal Reserve Bank of New York
NYSE: New York Stock Exchange
OFHEO: Office of Federal Housing Enterprise Oversight
OTC: over-the-counter (derivatives market)
PDCF: Primary Dealer Credit Facility
PLS: private-label (mortgage-backed) securities

PPIP: Public-Private Investment Program
REIT: real estate investment trust
ROA: return on assets
ROE: return on equity
RTC: Resolution Trust Corporation
S&L: savings and loan (institution)
SIV: special investment vehicle
SPV: special purpose vehicle
TALF: Term Auction Lending Facility
TARP: Troubled Asset Relief Program
TRIA: Terrorism Risk Insurance Act
TSLF: Term Securities Lending Facility
VA: Veteran's Administration (now the Department of Veterans Affairs)

INDEX